D0753717

INSIGHT ● GUIDES

SYDNEY

POCKET GUIDE

PLAN & BOOK
YOUR TAILOR-MADE TRIP

BRAZIL **CHILE** **ECUADOR**

TAILOR-MADE TRIPS & UNIQUE EXPERIENCES CREATED BY LOCAL TRAVEL EXPERTS AT INSIGHTGUIDES.COM/HOLIDAYS

Insight Guides has been inspiring travellers with high-quality travel content for over 45 years. As well as our popular guidebooks, we now offer the opportunity to book tailor-made private trips completely personalised to your needs and interests. By connecting with one of our local experts, you will directly benefit from their expertise and local know-how, helping you create memories that will last a lifetime.

HOW INSIGHTGUIDES.COM/HOLIDAYS WORKS

STEP 1

Pick your dream destination and submit an enquiry, or modify an existing itinerary if you prefer.

STEP 2

Fill in a short form, sharing details of your travel plans and preferences with a local expert.

STEP 3

Your local expert will create your personalised itinerary, which you can amend until you are completely satisfied.

STEP 4

Book securely online. Pack your bags and enjoy your holiday! Your local expert will be available to answer questions during your trip.

BENEFITS OF PLANNING & BOOKING AT INSIGHTGUIDES.COM/HOLIDAYS

PLANNED BY LOCAL EXPERTS

The Insight Guides local experts are hand-picked, based on their experience in the travel industry and their impeccable standards of customer service.

SAVE TIME & MONEY

When a local expert plans your trip, you save time and money when you book, even during high season. You won't be charged for using a credit card either.

TAILOR-MADE TRIPS

Book with Insight Guides, and you will be in complete control of the planning process, from the initial selections to amending your final itinerary.

BOOK & TRAVEL STRESS-FREE

Enjoy stress-free travel when you use the Insight Guides secure online booking platform. All bookings come with a money-back guarantee.

WHAT OTHER TRAVELLERS THINK ABOUT TRIPS BOOKED AT INSIGHTGUIDES.COM/HOLIDAYS

Trip to Vietnam

The organization was superb, the drivers professional, and accommodation quite comfortable. I was well taken care of! My thanks to your colleagues who helped make my trip to Vietnam such a great experience. My only regret is that I couldn't spend more time in the country.

Heather ★★★★★

DON'T MISS OUT BOOK NOW AT INSIGHTGUIDES.COM/HOLIDAYS

TOP 10 ATTRACTIONS

SYDNEY'S GLORIOUS HARBOUR
Venture out onto the water to explore the harbour. See page 28.

ART GALLERY OF NEW SOUTH WALES
Great displays of international, Aboriginal and modern Australian art. See page 42.

SYDNEY HARBOUR BRIDGE
An elegant work of art in grey steel. See page 36.

SYDNEY AQUARIUM
Where the Great Barrier Reef comes to the city. See page 53.

SYDNEY OPERA HOUSE
With its billowing sails and harbour setting, it's an architectural triumph. See page 39.

TARONGA ZOO
Among the inmates are koalas and kangaroos. See page 30.

ROYAL BOTANIC GARDENS
Lush and peaceful, with great harbour views. See page 41.

BLUE MOUNTAINS
Wilderness on the city's doorstep. See page 74.

THE ROCKS
The maritime-flavoured, historic heart of Sydney. See page 32.

BONDI BEACH
Not far from the city centre is Sydney's favourite ocean playground. See page 67.

A PERFECT DAY

8.00am

Breakfast

Start your day with breakfast in The Rocks or Circular Quay. Try La Renaissance Café Patisserie on Argyle Street, City Extra or Rossini on the Quay, or Pancakes on the Rocks on Hickson Road.

9.30am

Meet a koala

Hop on a ferry and cruise to Darling Harbour. At Sydney Wildlife World, you'll meet Australia's iconic animals, including koalas, wallabies, wombats and crocodiles.

1.30pm

Honour in Hyde Park

Stroll down Park Street to Hyde Park. Visit the moving Anzac Memorial to the country's fallen servicemen and women. At the other end of the park, the Archibald Fountain is an Art Deco delight.

11.30am

Shopping

Sydney is a great place to shop. The Queen Victoria Building may be the most beautiful shopping arcade in the world.

2.30pm

The Barracks

Opposite the fountain on Macquarie Street is the Hyde Park Barracks. It once housed prisoners, orphans and destitute women in Sydney's early years. The exhibits illustrate the grim conditions and how the survivors built the country.

IN SYDNEY

5.00pm

Art stroll
Take a short cab ride to Walsh Bay. Once a busy warehouse and dock area, it's the centre of Sydney's performing arts world. The Sculpture Walk features six head-turning sculptures. Relax with a drink at a waterside café as the sun sets. The area is currently undergoing a phased redevelopment to create a public arts and cultural hub.

10.30pm

On the town
Drink at one of the oldest pubs in Sydney. The Hero of Waterloo on George Street and the Lord Nelson Brewery both claim the title. Then view the city by night from Blu Bar on 36, atop the Shangri-La Hotel in The Rocks.

3.30pm

Great views
Cross back to Archibald Fountain, then turn right onto Market Street and the Sydney Tower Eye. From the observation deck (more than twice the height of the Sydney Harbour Bridge), you can see the Blue Mountains.

6.30pm

Dinner and a show
After a pre-theatre dinner, take in a show at the Opera House which is 'around the corner'. Other than the main theatre there are also performances in the Drama Theatre and Playhouse.

CONTENTS

INTRODUCTION

Sunny, surf-fringed Sydney seems custom-built for outdoor enjoyment. Bold, bright and alluring, the city glows with instant sensuous appeal, from the grey-green, eucalyptus-filled valleys on the city's outskirts to the terracotta-tiled roofs and swimming pools of the urban landscape.

The city's glorious harbour, stretching about 20km (12½miles) inland from the Pacific Ocean to the east, is its dominant feature, and was what induced the commanders of the first convict fleet to make their settlement here. The city is now a sprawling metropolis extending more than 40km (25 miles) west, 20km (12 miles) south and 15km (9miles) north of the harbour. The urban area is surrounded on all sides by vast national parks, most notably the Blue Mountains National Park to the west.

Just over 5 million people, a fifth of Australia's population, live in Sydney and it is regularly ranked as one of the world's favourite tourist destinations and city with the highest quality of living. It's easy to see why – if the world had a lifestyle capital, Sydney would be a strong contender. The city seamlessly combines all the advantages of big-city living – a vibrant arts and leisure scene, cultural diversity, world-class cuisine and spectacular architecture – with the easily accessible natural beauty of

Harbour views

Melbourne and Sydney enjoy a generally genial rivalry about their cities. Melbourne residents sometimes accuse Sydneysiders of being obsessed with finding housing with a view of the water. In a city where housing is already expensive, a two-bedroom flat with a glimpse of the harbour starts at a cool AU$1 million.

the surrounding harbour, beaches and green bush land. Moreover, Sydney's climate is pleasant and temperate for most of the year, seldom falling below 10°C (50°F) during the day in winter, with an average summer maximum of about 25°C (77°F).

Sydney Opera House

DIVERSE CITYSCAPE

Sydney Harbour, officially called Port Jackson, divides the city into north and south, with the great grey Harbour Bridge (completed in 1932) spanning the divide. Directly south of the bridge is Sydney's Central Business District (CBD), around which many of the city's key attractions – the Opera House, the historic Rocks district, Darling Harbour – are clustered. This area also hosts some of Sydney's most acclaimed restaurants, best shopping malls and premier arts venues.

Also to the south of the harbour, the eastern districts of Kings Cross and Paddington range from sleazy to gentrified and offer the best nightlife in the city. The beaches to the east of here include the famous Bondi. To the west, Chinatown and the Italian quarter of Leichhardt offer cheap eats, and further west still are the suburbs where most of Sydney's inhabitants live.

The landscapes north of the bridge are leafy, suburban and affluent, offering excellent views of the city and lovely beaches, from Manly on the edge of the harbour up to Palm Beach, about 40km (25 miles) from the CBD.

Surfers at Bondi

THE OUTDOOR LIFE

Sydneysiders (as the city's residents are known) make the most of their favourable surroundings and climate and delight in outdoor activities. The city's sports facilities are top-class and received a further boost when Sydney hosted the Olympics in 2000. Sydneysiders play and watch a panoply of sports including cricket, rugby league, Aussie Rules football, horseracing, swimming, surfing and yachting.

If you enjoy beach life, Sydney is for you. The shoreline is convoluted and would extend for some 350km (218 miles) if drawn out in a straight line. Along the coast and within the harbour, the city has dozens of beaches, all of which are open to the public. The beaches occupy a special position in the Sydney psyche, and each has a distinct character. Some are crowded and boisterous; others are secluded and little-known, found only after hiking along wooded trails. They can be divided into two main types: ocean beaches, which face out to sea and have stronger surf, and the more tranquil harbour beaches, which line Sydney Harbour.

SYDNEYSIDERS

Sydneysiders are a friendly and informal bunch. Old class distinctions were largely wiped out by the harsh realities of the colony's early history, where a person's skills and abilities became more important than anything else. However, beneath their 'no worries' approach, Sydneysiders have energy, ambition, belief and an overwhelming pride in their city. In the 1970s, when development projects threatened some of the city's most cherished historic or environmentally sensitive sites, builders' unions instituted 'green bans', where members refused to carry out any destructive work. Similarly, the overwhelming success of the 2000 Olympics was largely down to the enthusiasm and drive of the city's people.

The cultural and ethnic mix of that population is constantly evolving thanks to successive waves of immigration. The influence of the original British immigrants is still very much in evidence. Students at some of Sydney's private schools wear blazers and straw boaters just like their counterparts in Britain, cricket is played on local greens, and lawyers wear flowing black gowns and wigs at the Supreme Court.

The opening up of Australia since the end of World War II to immigration from has transformed Sydney into a modern, multicultural haven.

Immigrant city

The biggest sources of immigration into New South Wales are China, the UK, the Philippines, Lebanon, Vietnam, New Zealand, Italy and India. If current high levels of immigration continue, Sydney's population will reach 6.5 million by 2036.

A BRIEF HISTORY

What Sydney's history lacks in length, it makes up for in colour. In two centuries of existence, the city has had more than its share of characters – from tyrants such as Captain Bligh, notorious commander of the warship HMS *Bounty*, who survived a shipboard mutiny to find himself dispatched to Sydney as Governor of New South Wales, to the lesser-known figure James Hardy Vaux, a charming pickpocket and swindler, transported in chains from England to Australia three times. Each time Vaux managed to escape back to England, he was caught and sent back to Australia. Finally, there's respectable types like Bennelong, the first Aborigine to learn English and wear clothes.

A 1798 depiction of the founding of the colony

He travelled to London, where King George III gave him a coat. He returned to Sydney in 1795 and lived in a hut on the point where the Opera House now stands.

DREAMTIME ECHOES

Australia has been populated by modern humans for longer than Western Europe – possibly twice as long. Australia's original

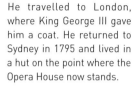

Aboriginal names

A number of locations in Sydney have Aboriginal names. Bondi means 'sound of rushing waters'; Coogee means 'rotten seaweed'; Ku-ring-gai is the name of the tribe that lived there; Cronulla means 'small pink shells' and Maroubra means 'rolling thunder'.

inhabitants are thought to have arrived between 40,000 and 60,000 years ago during the great Pleistocene Ice Age, crossing a land bridge from Southeast Asia. When Captain James Cook landed, the area around Sydney was inhabited by the Eora people, one of 600 or so Aboriginal tribes living in Australia. These tribes spoke many languages, some utterly dissimilar to one another. The word Eora, in the local Sydney-area language, simply meant 'here' or 'in this place'.

Aborigines lived within tribal boundaries they believed had been created by hero ancestors in a period called the Dreamtime. Dreamtime legends detail the significance of every tree, rock and river and explain how humans can live in harmony with nature; Aboriginal art expressed these and other spiritual beliefs. Trading paths and trails ran throughout Australia and were often invested with ceremonial or magical qualities. They connected waterholes, food sources and landmarks.

Aborigines built no permanent structures but lived in a way that ensured their survival in an often harsh environment. They foraged, fished and hunted kangaroo, wallaby, goanna lizards and

First Government House, by John Eyre

other native beasts with spears and boomerangs. They ate berries, roots and insects such as the witchetty grub (a large white grub about the size of a finger) and the bogong moth; the latter roasted on open fires before consumption.

COLONISTS IN CHAINS

In 1770 renowned English navigator Captain Cook spied the hills of eastern Australia and, reminded of the landscapes of southern Wales, dubbed the land New South Wales. He landed on Australia's east coast and explored Botany Bay, a short distance south of where Sydney now stands and today the site of Sydney Airport's third runway. Cook claimed all the territory he charted for King George III. While the Dutch (and possibly the Spanish, Portuguese and Chinese) had visited Australia before him, Cook's arrival was to have the greatest effect.

The British soon decided that Australia was an ideal place to send its convicts. In the late 18th century, Britain's prisons were at bursting point, and when the American War of Independence inconveniently interrupted the orderly transportation of convicts to America and the Caribbean (where they were used as virtual slave labour on plantations), the government decided Sydney would make the perfect penal colony. Britain at one stage had declared that 223 offences were punishable by death (including the crime of 'breaking down the head or mound of any fish-pond');

in practice, however, people were hanged for only 25 of these, leaving plenty of convicts to be transported to one of the farthest-flung corners of its empire.

The first 'prisoner-colonists' arrived in 1788. Under the command of retired naval officer Captain Arthur Phillip, the First Fleet consisted of 11 vessels carrying 1,030 people, including 548 male and 188 female convicts. The convicts were repeat offenders; their crimes usually involved theft. None was a murderer though – for that, you were hanged.

After briefly visiting Botany Bay, Phillip anchored in Port Jackson (named but not visited by Cook) to the north, which he described as 'the finest harbour in the world'. The fleet sailed into the semicircular bay now known as Circular Quay. This they named Sydney Cove, after Thomas Townshend, Viscount Sydney, the Secretary of State for the Colonies.

The Eora on the shore showed no fear of the light-skinned for-eigners and their ships. But they were curious. A British officer, Captain Watkin Tench, describes how an Aboriginal man closely examined a white child's skin, hat and clothes, 'muttering to himself all the while'. Despite such friendly encounters, the British saw the Aborigines as uncivilised nomads and took possession of their lands without treaty or compensation.

In the first few months of its existence, the fledgling colony of petty thieves,

Irish influx

The transportation of convicts from Britain helped make Australia the most Irish country outside Ireland. After British troops crushed the Irish rebellion of 1798, thousands of suspected rebels were hanged, tortured or transported. In 1800, almost all white Australians were English by birth or ancestry. Just eight years later, more than 20 percent were Irish.

sailors and soldiers ran headlong into famine. Starvation threatened, but Britain continued to send new shiploads of colonists. It was not until the foundation of an agricultural colony in Parramatta (25km/15.5 miles to the west) in 1790 that the threat of starvation receded.

Back in Britain the Home Secretary, Lord Bathurst (a Sydney street is named after him), declared he wanted criminals to regard the threat of transportation to Australia as 'an object of real terror'. It was made clear to all that colonial Governor Phillip was authorised to summarily jail, flog or hang anyone in New South Wales. Britain sent a Second Fleet to Sydney in 1790 – then a Third. Merciless floggings with the cat-o'-nine-tails (generally administered about 40 lashes a time, but sometimes over 100) kept a semblance of order – even if the punishment sometimes killed the recipients.

RUM LEGACY

Relations with the Eora and other Aboriginal tribes soured as rum and diseases introduced from the West took their toll. By 1840 the tribal life of Sydney's Aborigines had been destroyed. Sydney's Aboriginal population dwindled to just a few hundred by the end of the 19th century, as many Aborigines fled their traditional lands. Today, about 1 percent of the city's population is Aboriginal.

When Governor Phillip retired, the military took over. The colony's top army officer, Major Francis Grose, cornered the rum market. His

Rum hospital

The construction of Sydney's first hospital on Macquarie Street in 1812 was financed by giving the builders a monopoly of the rum trade. One wing is now Parliament House, another is the Mint; Sydney Hospital stands on the site of the long-demolished middle wing.

troops, nicknamed the Rum Corps, made fortunes in liquor racketeering. Sydney became one of the hardest-drinking settlements in the world, addicted to fiery Brazilian *aguardiente* and cheap spirits distilled in Bengal. Tradesmen were frequently paid in rum.

London eventually sent out a harsh disciplinarian to shake up the rum-sodden militia. Captain William Bligh was famous well before his arrival, having been set adrift in a longboat after the notorious mutiny on the warship HMS *Bounty* in 1789. Rather than perish at sea as the mutineers had expected, Bligh and his 18 companions had sailed from Tahiti to Timor, a journey of about 6,400km (4,000 miles), one of the longest voyages ever accomplished in an open boat. When Bligh was appointed Governor of New South Wales in 1805, his legendary temper soon earned him the nickname Caligula, after one of the most hated and feared Roman emperors.

Captain Bligh

On 26 January 1808, as Bligh was toasting the 20th anniversary of Sydney's founding, a group of his officers mutinied and took him prisoner. The Rum Rebellion, as the uprising became known, deposed Bligh and held him under arrest for a year. London sent a talented Scottish officer, Lachlan Macquarie, to arrest the rebels. Bligh's career was unblemished by all this – he finished up a vice-admiral – but he lost the governorship of New South Wales to Macquarie.

MACQUARIE'S VISION

Life in the new colony improved under Macquarie's progressive administration, and Sydney began to look more like a real town than a military encampment. Thatched huts gave way to properly built schools, churches, a hospital and a courthouse. Francis Greenway, a convicted forger whom Macquarie had pardoned, became the colony's official architect. He turned out to be highly talented. His surviving buildings include St James's Church in King Street and Hyde Park Barracks. Many of Macquarie's reforms were resisted by London, which could not reconcile his civilising efforts with the original concept of creating a hellish environment that filled criminals with dread.

The transportation of prisoners continued halfway into the 19th century, but was eventually outpaced by free immigration. In 1849, when one of the last convict ships docked in Sydney Cove, its presence provoked outrage among Sydney's 'respectable' citizens. The ship arrived at the same time as several other vessels carrying free immigrants. Even so, the descendants of convicts

⊙ THE BUSHRANGERS

Highway robbers, horse thieves and assorted outlaws fanned out across Australia in the 1850s, and the gold rush served to raise the stakes. Among the most notorious was Ned Kelly. A one-time cattle rustler, Kelly and his gang pulled off spectacular robberies, mostly in Victoria. His most memorable incursion into New South Wales was in 1879, when the gang kidnapped the population of the town of Jerilderie while trying to make a getaway after a bank robbery. A year later, an unrepentant Ned Kelly went to the gallows. 'Such is life,' were Ned's reputed last words.

outnumbered free settlers in Sydney until well into the 20th century.

THE GOLD RUSH

In the 19th century, fortune smiled on Australia. In 1813, explorers crossed the Blue Mountains to the west of Sydney and found a land of endless plains – dry country, but arable. In 1851, beyond the Blue Mountains and 200km (130 miles) from Sydney, a veteran of the California gold rush struck gold at a settlement named Ophir.

Hyde Park Barracks, designed by Francis Greenway

The gold rush helped shape the history of modern Australia, reversing the exodus of Australians to the California goldfields and bringing an influx of new settlers to the Australian colonies. In 1851, the population of New South Wales was just 187,000. Nine years later it had nearly doubled, to 348,000.

Shortly after the Ophir bonanza, prospectors from Melbourne struck gold at Ballarat, triggering an invasion of adventurers from Europe and America, which lifted Australia's population to 1 million by 1860. Life in the goldfields was rough and uncompromising. Miners endured flies, heat, water shortages and extortionate taxes. Hundreds of prospectors arrived in Australia from China, unleashing local racist sentiment, which endured well into the 20th century. Racially based immigration controls – the infamous White Australia Policy – remained in force from 1901 to 1972.

The halves of the bridge's arch finally met on 19 August 1930

A NATION EMERGES

Australia's island continent remained a collection of separate colonies until 1 January 1901, when Queen Victoria permitted the colonies to unite and form a new nation, the Commonwealth of Australia. The new country bowed to the Queen as head of state, and its final legal authority rested with the British sovereign's private council in London. Although the latter arrangement has changed, Britain's monarch is still Australia's head of state and is depicted on all coinage. Britain's Union flag dominates Australia's flag.

Australia has yet to become a republic, and, in a referendum in 1999, the proposed model for such a state system was rejected, due to concern that it would grant politicians too much power. Australians considered themselves British until well into the 20th century. In World War I, Australian and New Zealand troops formed the Australian and New Zealand Army

Corps (Anzac) to fight alongside other British Empire sol-
diers. On 25 April 1915, the Anzacs landed at Gallipoli (now in
Turkey) in an ill-conceived operation that cost the lives of 8,700
Australians, with 19,000 wounded. More than 60,000 Australian
soldiers died in World War I, with 152,000 wounded. No other
country suffered as high a loss in proportion to its population.
The carnage had a major effect on Australia's psyche. Anzac
Day, 25 April, is a national day of remembrance.

THE IRON LUNG

Between the wars, Sydney devoted its energies to building
the Harbour Bridge, which gained the nickname 'iron lung'
because its building took hundreds of workers and kept families breathing (in financial terms) during the Depression.

In World War II, Japanese warplanes repeatedly bombed
Darwin in Australia's north, enemy submarines penetrated
Sydney Harbour in 1942 and sank a ferry (the torpedo had been
fired at an American warship), ships were sunk off the New South
Wales coast, and a couple of shells hit Sydney's eastern suburbs.
Almost one in three Australians taken prisoner by the Japanese
died in captivity. American forces under General Douglas
MacArthur arrived in Australia in 1942, and a US force supported
by Australia defeated the Japanese decisively in the Battle of the
Coral Sea in May of that year.

After the war, Britain aligned itself with Europe and downgraded
its ties with the old empire. As Britain's regional power declined,
Australia looked increasingly to the US. Australian troops (over
40,000 of them) fought alongside the US in Vietnam, sparking
vehement anti-war protests in Sydney and other Australian cities. Australian Prime Minister Harold Holt promised US President
Lyndon B. Johnson that Australia would go 'all the way with LBJ'.
The alliance with the US has remained close, and Australia has

contributed troops to wars in Iraq, Syria and Afghanistan. Today this alliance remains Australia's most important defence.

A WORLD CITY

High immigration and rising affluence fed Sydney's post-war expansion. From 1.8 million in 1951, Sydney's population reached 2.7 million in 1971, 3.2 million in 1981 and over 5 million in 2018. New suburbs were built, especially in the west, while older inner-city districts such as Paddington and Surry Hills declined. From the late 1950s, successive building booms reshaped the CBD and created a mini-CBD at North Sydney. Many historic buildings were demolished, replaced by skyscrapers. Later, the gentrification of inner-city suburbs, led by Paddington in the 1970s, saw the rush to the outer suburbs subside to some extent.

Sydney changed its face, but one building stood out. In 1959, construction of the Sydney Opera House began. Although its architect, Jørn Utzon, resigned in 1966 with the shell incomplete, the building opened to acclaim in 1973.

By the 1980s, Sydney had supplanted Melbourne's role as Australia's main financial centre. Tourism increased significantly, as evidenced by the redevelopment of Darling Harbour in the mid-1980s. Australia's bicentennial celebrations in 1988 focused on Sydney. And the successful staging of the Olympics in 2000 symbolised Sydney's new status as a world city. Although these changes haven't been without cost – disparities between rich and poor have grown, and traffic congestion is increasing – economic conditions, boosted by the Australian mining boom, were good, and Sydney's mood remained buoyant. In 2013–14 Sydney's economy grew by 4.3 percent, its fastest growth in 14 years. Since then the city's economy has slowed to a stable growth rate which varies between 2 and 3 percent year on year.

HISTORICAL LANDMARKS

c.60,000BC Aborigines migrate to Australia from southern Asia.

AD1606 Dutch navigator Willem Jansz lands in Cape York.

1688 English pirate William Dampier visits Australia's west coast.

1770 James Cook claims New South Wales for Britain.

1788 First Fleet of British convicts and soldiers arrives.

1808 Governor William Bligh deposed in Rum Rebellion.

1809 Governor Lachlan Macquarie appointed.

1849 Transportation of convicts to New South Wales ends.

1851 Gold discovered near Bathurst.

1860s Melbourne overtakes Sydney as Australia's largest city.

1898 Queen Victoria Building completed.

1901 Britain allows its Australian colonies to unify into one nation.

1905 Sydney overtakes Melbourne as Australia's largest city.

1915 Anzac soldiers storm ashore at Gallipoli in military disaster.

1932 Height of the Great Depression (unemployment rate is 32 percent); Sydney Harbour Bridge opens.

1942 Japanese midget submarines penetrate Sydney Harbour.

1946 Australia conceives 'Populate or Perish' immigration programme.

1955 Arrival of Australia's 1-millionth post-war migrant.

1962 Aborigines given right to vote in federal elections.

1973 Sydney Opera House opens.

1975 The Governor General sacks Australia's elected Prime Minister.

1988 Bicentenary of arrival of First Fleet.

2000 Sydney Olympic and Paralympic Games.

2001 Centenary of Federation.

2007 Sydney Opera House added to the Unesco World Heritage List.

2008 Federal government apologises to Aborigines for past wrongs.

2010 Hyde Park Barracks added to the Unesco World Heritage List.

2014 A 17-hour siege by Iranian-born Man Haron Monis in Lindt Café claims three lives, including his own.

2018 Sydney's population reaches five million.

2019 The first stage of Sydney Metro, Sydney Metro Northwest, is completed.

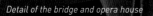
Detail of the bridge and opera house

WHERE TO GO

Sydney is a big, sprawling city. It stretches some 75km (45 miles) from north to south and 65km (40 miles) from east to west. Fortunately for visitors, most of Sydney's essential sights are close together, just south of the Harbour Bridge. As well as the bridge itself, these include The Rocks, the Sydney Opera House, the Royal Botanic Gardens, the CBD and Darling Harbour. All are accessible on foot or by bus or train.

A short bus or train ride gets you to the trendy neighbourhoods of the Inner West, and the beaches (including Bondi), café culture and shopping opportunities of the Eastern Suburbs. Circular Quay, also south of the bridge, is the main ferry terminal, and a jumping-off point for exploring the wonders of Sydney Harbour.

Accessible by train or on an organised tour are western Sydney's Olympic Park (site of the 2000 Olympics), Featherdale Wildlife Park and Parramatta, which can also be reached by ferry. To the north, Taronga Zoo, Manly and the Northern Beaches can be reached by ferry or bus.

Sydney has several great natural attractions on its doorstep. The Blue Mountains, about 100km (60 miles) to the west, make an unmissable day trip, either by car, by train or as part of an organised tour. Those with time to spare might also like to consider an excursion to the Jenolan Caves, the Hunter Valley, the Southern Highlands and the Hawkesbury River.

Aerial views

One way to see the harbour at its best is to fly over it. A number of companies offer scenic flights. Try Sydney Helicopters (tel: 02 9637-4455) or Sydney by Seaplane (tel: 1300 720 995).

Also included in this book is Canberra, about 300km (185 miles) southwest of Sydney, which is Australia's capital city and the location of some of the country's finest galleries and museums.

SYDNEY HARBOUR

The harbour is the city's essence – spanned by the great bridge and adorned by the shell-like sails of Sydney Opera House. Sydneysiders flock to the harbour to celebrate great events. They turned out here to greet Queen Elizabeth II on her first visit to Australia in 1954, and they were here again in January 1988 to celebrate the bicentenary of the First Fleet's arrival, which marked the founding of modern Australia.

New Year celebrations take place in the historic Rocks area near the southern end of Sydney Harbour Bridge. Tens of thousands of people turn out to watch a massive fireworks display that has the bridge as its focal point. Each Boxing Day, thousands of Sydneysiders line the harbour to watch the start of the gruelling Sydney to Hobart yacht race.

The best way to see **Sydney Harbour** ❶ is to get out on it. Sydney Ferries runs numerous public ferries from Circular Quay (called Sydney Cove in the days of convict settlement), providing a fast and cheap means of seeing the city's most attractive aspects. In addition to being vital links for commuters, the ferries are bargains for tourists. Sydney Ferries' website has an easy-to-read map of the ferry system. Signage at the wharf is also easy to follow, and staff are used to directing confused tourists to the right boat. A number of private companies also offer cruises. Itineraries range from hour-long 'best of' trips to lunch and dinner cruises and high-speed circuits of the harbour in jet boats. One of the leading tour boat companies is Captain Cook Cruises (tel: 02 9206-1111; www.captaincook.com.au).

Aerial view of the harbour and a jet boat

Its 'Harbour Explorer Hop-On Hop-Off' 2-day pass allows 10 stops at five harbour attractions. Harbour Explorer pass Hop On Hop Off rocket ferries depart from Circular Quay and Darling Harbour. You can also set sail on a tall ship (tel: 02 8015-5571; www.sydneytallships.com.au) or go for an invigorating spin on a fast jet boat (tel: 1300-887-373; www.harbourjet.com or tel: 02 9808-3700; www.ozjetboating.com).

HARBOUR HIGHLIGHTS

Exploring Sydney Harbour is as easy as hopping on a ferry. Popular destinations include Taronga Zoo (see page 30), Cremorne Point (see page 32), Darling Harbour (see page 50), Balmain (see page 62), Parramatta (see page 65), Watsons Bay (see page 69) and Manly (see page 71).

Sydney Harbour National Park fringes a long stretch of the northern side of the harbour and also includes some harbour

Koala at Taronga Zoo

islands and a chunk of the southern foreshore. Walking tracks lead through bushland remnants, past waterfront mansions and along harbour beaches.

Fort Denison, part of Sydney Harbour National Park, occupies a small harbour island known as 'Pinchgut', which originally served as a prison. Troublesome convicts endured a bread-and-water diet and sometimes even worse. In 1796, a murderer was executed by hanging on the island and his body gibbeted for three years as a warning. Fort Denison contains a martello tower (a circular masonry blockhouse), a barracks and gun battery, all dating from the 1850s. The fort is open for guided tours only (tel: 1300 072 757; www.nationalparks.nsw. gov.au/things-to-do/historic-buildings-places/fort-denison; currently closed for maintenance, check website for details).

Taronga Zoo ❷ (www.taronga.org.au; daily 9.30am–5pm) is just 12 minutes from the city by ferry. There is a 'ZooPass' available which includes the ferry ticket, admission to the zoo and a sky safari ride. Most tourists have their first encounter with Australian Wildlife at Taronga, situated in natural bush land at Bradleys Head, Mosman. The setting can't be beaten; if you choose your vantage point carefully, you can photograph the heads of giraffes against a background of the CBD cityscape, including the Opera House. Visitors can download a map from the zoo's website for a self-guided walk through the zoo, or, for more direction, there is a variety of guided tours. If you arrange your visit around feeding times (which are on the website) you can watch the keepers distribute food while they deliver talks about their charges. Visitors are encouraged to explore the Rainforest Trail with its range of Southeast Asian species, and Great Southern Oceans, which showcase the great diversity of the southern seas including seals, penguins and pelicans. Taronga also offers a breathtaking free flight bird show on a cliff overlooking Sydney Harbour and a seal show, both twice daily.

Other parts of Sydney Harbour worth seeing are **Balmoral Beach**, near Mosman, with shops and cafés along the beachfront Esplanade, and **Kirribilli**, just across the harbour from Circular Quay and accessible by ferry, train (to Milsons Point

◎ WEIRD WADDLERS

The echidna and platypus displays at Taronga Zoo allow you to view these reclusive Australian monotremes (egg-laying mammals) close up. The waddling, spine-covered echidnas dine on ants and termites. The duck-billed platypus is even more peculiar, having astonished observers since explorers first laid eyes on it. When 18th-century zoologists in London received their first stuffed and preserved specimens, they doubted anything that weird could exist. Most experts considered it a composite fake, assembled by Chinese taxidermists for sale to gullible seafarers. The platypus is the size of a small cat, with a broad bill and webbed feet like a duck. It is amphibious, covered in fine fur, possesses milk-secreting glands, lays eggs and dines exclusively on mud, from which it extracts tiny plants and animals. The platypus was not declared a mammal until 1884.

station) or on foot across the Harbour Bridge. This elegant residential area includes the Sydney residences of the Prime Minister and Governor General of Australia.

One particularly lovely short walk on the Lower North Shore starts from the ferry wharf at **Cremorne Point** – where there are fine views of the city and harbour – and winds along the shore of Mosman Bay to the wharf at Mosman. The pleasant walk takes about 1.5 hours.

HARBOURSIDE ATTRACTIONS

CIRCULAR QUAY AND THE ROCKS

Circular Quay is frequented by buskers, artists and street performers. Circular Quay railway station provides quick connections to Kings Cross and to points in the centre of the city, as well as to the outlying suburbs. The Quay (as it's often called) is a major bus terminal, and it is an easy place to hail a cab.

The Rocks ❸, just west of Circular Quay, is touristy and souvenir-dominated in some parts, quaint and fascinating in others. The birthplace of Sydney – the First Fleet ended its journey from England here in 1788 – this district was a squalid slum in the 19th century, harbouring an evil gang of cut-throats known as The Rocks Push. Many of the district's original houses were torn down in 1900, when the area was hit by an outbreak of bubonic plague. It killed nearly 100 people. Plenty of historic buildings survived, only to be threatened in the 1960s by developers wanting to level the whole place and replace it with high-rise buildings. A 'Save The Rocks' campaign, backed by the union movement, only just prevailed.

It's worth visiting the **Sydney Visitor Centre** (tel: 02-8273-0000; daily 9.30am–5.30pm), on the corner of Argyle and Playfair streets, before setting out to explore. Displays and pamphlets provide insights into the area's history. **Cadman's Cottage** (110 George Street) is The Rocks' oldest house, a simple stone cottage built in 1816. The cottage is now administered by the National Parks & Wildlife Service. Sydney's Big Dig (between Cumberland and Gloucester streets) contains the foundations of over 30 homes and shops from as early as

An Aboriginal busker

1795. The Sydney Youth Hostel is built above the site on raised columns, which allows visitors to see the excavation while protecting it (www.thebigdig.com.au).

A short stroll from the visitor centre, the **Museum of Contemporary Art** (www.mca.com.au; daily 10am–5pm) gives new life to an Art Deco building formerly used by the Maritime Services Board.

Displays change regularly at the museum, and the café on the terrace facing Circular Quay and the harbour is excellent and offers a superb view.

Walking north from Cadman's Cottage up Argyle Street you arrive at the so-called **Argyle Cut**, a road carved through sandstone cliffs. It was started in 1843 by convict gangs using pickaxes and finished 18 years later by non-convict labour using explosives. At the top of Argyle Cut, Cumberland Street provides access to Sydney Harbour Bridge via Cumberland Steps. Beer connoisseurs

The Rocks Market

will enjoy the range of beers available at the bar at the Australian Hotel, 100 Cumberland Street (see page 135).

A little further on, in Argyle Place, you will find a neat row of terraced houses straight out of Georgian England. This area is called Millers Point and, with its tree-lined streets, street-corner pubs and old houses, has a less touristy, more relaxed feel to it than The Rocks. Three grand old pubs in this area deserve mention. The quaint Hero of Waterloo at 81 Lower Fort Street was built on top of a maze of subterranean cellars to which drunken patrons were reputedly lured, to be sold as crew members to unscrupulous sea captains. That practice has died out, but the cellars remain. The Lord Nelson, a square sandstone block of a building at the corner of Kent and Argyle streets, opened in 1831 to serve seafarers and dock workers, and has maintained a British naval atmosphere ever since. A pioneer in the Australian craft brewery movement, it is known for its line of ales which are brewed on-site.

For history without the refreshments, visit the **Garrison Church**, officially named the Holy Trinity Anglican Church, which dates from the early 1840s. As the unofficial name indicates, it was the church for members of the garrison regiment, the men in charge of the convict colony. It's now a fashionable place to get married.

To the left of the church, up a flight of stone stairs, is Observatory Park, which gives views to Darling Harbour and Balmain. **Sydney Observatory** ❹ (tel: 02 9217-0111; www. maas.museum/sydney-observatory; daily 10am–5pm) has displays about meteorology and astronomy. The night viewing sessions use the Observatory's telescope to view the night sky. Night viewing sessions hours vary depending on season (reservations required by phone or online). Walk north down Lower Fort Street and you will come to Dawes Point Park, beneath the arch of the Harbour Bridge. Go down to the harbour foreshore for views, and then follow the foreshore around to the converted cargo wharves of **Walsh Bay**, a dynamic cultural area, home to the Sydney Theatre, Bangarra Dance Theatre, Sydney Dance Company, Australian Theatre for Young People and the Wharf Theatre. These theatres have temporarily relocated due to redevelopment of the area. When complete, the wharf will once again house many cafés and restaurants offering terrific views across the bay.

The Rocks Market (www.therocks.com; Fri 9am–6pm, Sat–Sun 10am–5pm), held every weekend along George and Playfair streets, features over 200 vendors. On Fridays the emphasis is on food, with stalls enticing passers-by with sizzling lamb kebabs, Moroccan wraps and Bavarian sausages. In the summer, it's a street party, with live music after dark. On Saturday and Sunday, vendors sell unique homeware, fashion, music and artwork. This is the place to find unique Australian gifts and souvenirs at reasonable prices:

Suez Canal

The lanes through to The Rocks were once inhabited by bandits. Suez Canal, perhaps the most ominous of these, cuts between Harrington and George Street.

vintage Australian licence plates, food and spices from the Outback, hand-knitted clothing, even Christmas ornaments.

SYDNEY HARBOUR BRIDGE

With its drive-through stone pylons and colossal steel arch, **Sydney Harbour Bridge** ❺ triumphantly spans the harbour and is a sight to behold.

Before the Sydney Opera House opened in 1973, the bridge was the most internationally recognised symbol of Sydney. Completed in 1932, the bridge was to have been opened by the Premier of New South Wales, but just as that worthy gentleman approached the official ribbon brandishing his pair of golden scissors, an unauthorised horseman rode through the crowd and slashed the ribbon in two with a sabre. The mounted protestor, a member of a right-wing paramilitary group, declared the bridge open in the name of 'the decent citizens of New South Wales'. It was a bizarre initiation for a Sydney icon that was intended to be the world's longest single-span bridge – it was beaten just four months before its opening by New York's Bayonne Bridge, which is just 63cm (2ft) longer.

Sydney Harbour Bridge, nicknamed 'The Coathanger', took nine years to build. It was one of the foremost engineering

⊙ SYDNEY WRITERS WALK

A series of 49 manhole-sized brass plaques are embedded into the walkway around Circular Quay. This is Sydney Writers Walk, which honours well-known and obscure Australian writers as well as non-Aussies who lived in, visited or commented upon the country. Each plaque includes a brief passage of the author's work and biographical information.

Sydney Harbour Bridge

feats of its day. Some 1,400 workers toiled on the 503m (1,651ft) structure. Sixteen lost their lives. Repainting the bridge is a 10-year job, using 30,000 litres (almost 7,000 UK gallons) of paint. Once finished, it's time to start again. Paul 'Crocodile Dundee' Hogan worked on this monotonous task for years before discovering there was more money – and more satis-faction – in show business.

The bridge is equipped with a pedestrian walkway, a cycle lane, road lanes and a railway line. For a small fee, you can climb the 200 stairs inside the southeast pylon for panoramic views (tel: 02 9240-1100; www.pylonlookout.com.au; daily 10am–5pm). The pylon's museum includes displays about the engineering of the bridge, memorabilia and six stained-glass windows honouring the labourers who built the bridge. The pylon is reached via a stairway on Cumberland Street in The Rocks.

The bridge is the focal point for Sydney's New Year's Eve celebrations. The numbers for the countdown to the New Year appear on the bridge's pylons. As the New Year begins, some 1,600 rockets are fired from the arch in sequence, while other fireworks positioned on the road span create a cascade into Sydney Harbour.

The bridge's role is less crucial now that you can drive under the harbour through a tunnel. The tunnel trip is faster but boring. Guided climbing tours of the bridge now allow you to walk right over the huge overarching span (see page 91).

For a nice scenic walk, take the 30-minute stroll over the bridge to the delightful harbourside suburb of **Kirribilli**, whose tree-lined streets – some of which face the Opera House – invite exploration. Refresh yourself in one of the numerous cafés and restaurants here before returning to the city.

SYDNEY OPERA HOUSE

Standing on the western side of Circular Quay and gazing east, the viewer is confronted by one of Sydney's most beautiful buildings,

⊘ BATS ALOFT

The large flocks of bats flitting through Sydney skies often startle visitors, but they are not an invasion from a horror movie. They are grey-headed flying foxes. Weighing up to 1kg (2.2 pounds), the bats fly over the city at dusk to dine on figs and other soft fruit. Watching a flock on the wing, silhouetted against an awesome orange and mauve sunset, is one of Sydney's priceless experiences. The bats, with their furry, foxy faces, frequent the Royal Botanic Gardens (especially the palm grove) and Centennial Park, but their main camp is at Gordon, a leafy suburb on Sydney's North Shore.

the **Sydney Opera House** ❻ (www.sydneyoperahouse.com). Covered in a million gleaming white tiles, this extraordinary building does the seemingly impossible and embellishes a perfect harbour. While it's hard to imagine the harbour without it, the Opera House nearly wasn't built at all. The design was one of 233 entries submitted in a contest to find an ideal building for the site, which had previously been occupied by a squat, turreted depot for trams.

As the contest progressed, several banal entries (including one resembling two giant shoeboxes) were shortlisted. Danish architect Jørn Utzon's vision for the site, the eventual winner, was at first discarded. Fortunately, Utzon's plan was spotted by accident in a pile of rejects by US architect Eero Saarinen, one of the judges. Saarinen recognised the plan's potential and brought it to the attention of his colleagues.

Utzon moved to Sydney to oversee construction, but endless bickering with petty officials and enormous cost overruns took

There are over 50,000 plants in the Royal Botanic Gardens

their toll, and he resigned from the project in 1966, returning disillusioned to Denmark. The interior plan was subsequently handed over to a committee of Australian architects. Utzon never returned to see the finished work.

In 1999 he agreed to be a consultant with his architect son, Jan, in drawing up a statement of design principles that will help guide Australian architect Richard Johnson on future development works. The first is the Utzon Room, used for functions and small-scale concerts and a colonnade along the Harbour Bridge side of the Opera House. The refurbishment of the interior of the main performance halls and other upgrades are planned, but the timetable depends on funding.

The Opera House was originally budgeted at AU$7 million, but ended up costing 13 times that. In true Sydney style, the shortfall was raised by a lottery. Despite its cost, the finished project was immediately hailed for its grace, taste and class.

Elegance extends from the tip of its highest shell-like roof, which soars 67m (221ft), to the Drama Theatre's orchestra pit, situated several metres below sea level.

Strictly speaking, the term Opera House is a misnomer. The building's opera theatre (seating 1,547) is fairly small and not entirely satisfactory, although its intimacy helps some productions. Its concert hall (seating 2,697) is the biggest of five halls, and stages rock and jazz concerts as well as classical music. The Opera House offers a spectacular restaurant Bennelong and Opera Bar. It's worth taking a guided tour of the whole building. The one-hour tours depart every 30 minutes from 9am to 5pm each day, except for Christmas Day and Good Friday (advanced booking is recommended).

Back towards Circular Quay is the colonnaded Opera Quays pedestrian link between Circular Quay and the Opera House. The cafés, restaurants, shops and art-house cinema lining the way are lively additions to the Sydney scene.

ROYAL BOTANIC GARDENS

Situated next to the Opera House, Sydney's lush **Royal Botanic Gardens** ❼ (established in 1816) offer an extensive collection of Pacific plant life, a tropical garden, palm grove, lawns, a restaurant and café tucked away in the greenery and some wonderful picnic spots (www.rbgsyd.nsw.gov.au; daily 7am–sunset). A sign in the gardens is worth quoting: 'Please walk on the grass. We also invite you to smell the roses, hug the trees, talk to the birds, sit on the benches and picnic on the lawns. This is your Garden, and unlike most botanic gardens overseas, admission to the Royal Botanic Gardens is free.' (A slot for donations is provided however and goes towards the upkeep of the gardens). There are free daily 90-minute guided walking tours (at 10.30am), with one-hour tours weekdays from Mar–Nov at 1pm. You can also pay to go on the

The oldest pub

There's a lively debate about which pub is the oldest in Sydney. The arguments hinge on dates licences were issued, pedigree of ownership, location, when it was named, and personal bias. The contenders – all within a boomerang's toss of each other – are The Fortune of War, The Lord Nelson, The Hero of Waterloo and the Australian Hotel.

trackless train, which winds its way through the gardens on a 25-minute narrated tour.

Sublime views of Sydney Harbour can be enjoyed in the Royal Botanic Gardens from **Mrs Macquarie's Chair**, a sandstone rock ledge carved in 1816 for the wife of Sydney's best-loved governor. Mrs Macquarie's Chair stands beside Mrs Macquarie's Road on Mrs Macquarie's Point. (You couldn't go far wrong in early 19th-century Sydney by naming geographical features after the governor's wife.) The view from Mrs Macquarie's Chair, looking west across Farm Cove to the Opera House, is one of the world's most photographed. Here, nature and architecture meld beautifully, with the Royal Botanic Gardens forming a perfect backdrop to the Opera House.

Beside the gardens, and separated from them by the Cahill Expressway, is **The Domain ❽**, another of Sydney's wonderful open spaces. Given over to amateur orators on Sundays (rather like Speakers' Corner in London's Hyde Park), The Domain is also home to the **Art Gallery of New South Wales ❾** (tel: 1800-679-278; www.artgallery.nsw.gov.au; daily 10am–5pm, Wed until 10pm). The museum boasts one of the finest collections of Australian, Aboriginal, Torres Strait Islander, European, Asian and contemporary art in the country. The expansive, light-filled galleries for contemporary art also offer views of Sydney and the harbour, while the Grand Courts display the Old

Masters of Europe and 19th-century Australian work in a more appropriate setting. There are separate galleries dedicated to Asian art and work by Aboriginal and Torres Strait Islander art. As part of its commitment to support art in all its forms, the gallery also hosts a full schedule of lectures and symposia, films, music and performances.

Chiswick at the Gallery is a lovely casual venue that is open for lunch daily and for dinner on Wednesdays. It features a large communal table and offers views of Woolloomooloo and Sydney Harbour.

CENTRAL SYDNEY

Sydney's city centre, universally called the **CBD** (Central Business District), includes a magnificently restored late 19th-century emporium, several elegant Georgian sandstone edifices, some fine Victorian structures and a vast number of high-rise buildings. A few recent skyscrapers are notable and some are even elegant, but most belong to the so-called 'international egg-crate' school of architecture – bland modern buildings that were erected mainly in the 1960s and 1970s.

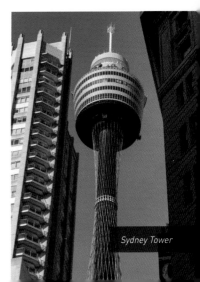

Sydney Tower

Stained glass in the QVB

GEORGE, PITT AND MARKET STREETS

George Street, running north–south, is the city's main thoroughfare. Parallel to it is Pitt Street, which is pedestrian-only between Market and Castlereagh streets. Together, this area makes up Sydney's main shopping district. Myer and David Jones, the two major Australian depart-ment stores can be found in **Pitt Street Mall**. Shopping complexes include the Imperial Arcade, Centrepoint, Skygarden and Glasshouse. The **Strand Arcade**, which runs between Pitt Street Mall and George Street, is a Victorian shopping arcade with some very up-to-the-minute boutiques. George Street is currently undergoing one of the biggest transformations ever seen in Sydney to incorporate the Sydney Light Rail.

At 309m (1014ft), **Sydney Tower** ❿ (www.sydneytowereye. com.au; daily 9am–9pm) at Centrepoint is the city's highest van-tage point. Visitors get a 360-degree view of the city and beyond, including the Harbour Bridge, Blue Mountains, Botany Bay and the Pacific Ocean. Admission to the observation deck includes a 15-minute virtual tour of Australia via a 'live motion' surround sound theatre. Wheelchair patrons are accommodated on the observation deck, provided the tower has 48 hours' notice and there is an able-bodied carer. The truly fearless can opt for the 45-min-long outdoor skywalk tour on a glass-bottomed platform

twice as high as the Harbour Bridge (www.sydneytowereye.com.
au; daily 9.30am–8.45pm; currently closed, check website for
updates). There is a combination ticket available which includes
the Tower, the Sydney Aquarium, Sydney Wildlife World and
Madame Tussauds Sydney.

Walk north on George or Pitt streets to reach the city's
main square, **Martin Place**, flanked by the imposing Victorian
Renaissance-style General Post Office (GPO) building. No longer a
working post office, this structure has been converted into a 418-
room, five-star Westin hotel, with luxury and designer shops, and
upmarket restaurants, cafés and bars. During World War II, the
GPO's clock tower was dismantled for fear that Japanese bomb-
ers might zero in on the landmark; it was restored 20 years later.

From the same era as the GPO, but even grander, the **Queen
Victoria Building** ⓫ (QVB) occupies an entire block on George
Street opposite Sydney Town Hall. The Romanesque-style QVB
began as a municipal market and commercial centre. Built in 1898
to commemorate Queen Victoria's Golden Jubilee, this splendid
building was later downgraded into offices and a library. It was
faithfully restored in the 1980s to create a magnificent all-weather

⊙ SYDNEY FISH MARKET

The world's second-largest seafood market (the largest is in
Japan), the Sydney Fish Market auctions over 100 species of
seafood harvested from Australian and New Zealand waters
every day – 13,500 tonnes annually. The Sydney Seafood School
at the market started as a way to introduce consumers to un-
familiar varieties of fish and other seafood. It's morphed into
a leading cookery school, with over 12,000 participants signing
up each year for classes and demonstrations by leading chefs.

shopping centre housing nearly 200 chic boutiques, cafés and restaurants, in a cool and unhurried atmosphere of period charm. Glorious stained-glass windows honouring the craftspeople who built the structure accent the building's mighty centre dome, sheathed in gleaming copper outside and lined with glass. To experience an elegant high tea, visit The Tearoom on Level 3 (tel: 02 9283-7279; www.thetearoom.com.au; daily 10am–10pm).

Opposite the QVB on George Street is the Hilton Hotel. The modern concrete-and-glass Hilton building contains a hidden architectural gem in its basement. This is the **Marble Bar**, a Beaux-Arts masterpiece of a pub, much older than the Hilton itself. A cornucopia of Victorian paintings, stained glass, marble and mirrors, the Marble Bar was preserved when the 19th-century building it was part of was knocked down to make way for the Hilton in the 1970s.

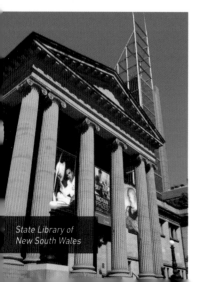

State Library of New South Wales

MACQUARIE'S SYDNEY

The CBD's only real boulevard is **Macquarie Street**, laid out by Governor Lachlan Macquarie and running from East Circular Quay near the Opera House to Hyde Park. This relatively short street, filled with historic buildings, is well worth the walk.

Starting at the northern end, Macquarie Street flanks **Government House**, which was the official residence of the Governor of

New South Wales from 1846–1996 (tel: 02 9228-4111; Fri–Sun for guided tours only 10.30am–3pm, occasionally closed for official functions; visitors are required to present valid identification). This extraordinary mock-Gothic castle, complete with crenellated battlements, was designed in 1834 by architect Edward Blore, who was also involved in designing Buckingham Palace. Until 1996 it was the official residence of the Governor of New South Wales.

Just off Macquarie Street, nestled beneath a modern skyscraper, is the **Museum of Sydney** (tel: 02 9251-5988; www.sydneylivingmuseums.com.au/museum-of-sydney; daily 10am–5pm), built on the site of the colony's first Government House. This small museum's permanent exhibits focus on the city's history from 1788 onwards, and regular temporary exhibitions are also staged.

The **State Library of New South Wales**, bordering The Domain, consists of two buildings linked by a walkway. Classical columns announce the main portal of the old Mitchell Wing, built in Greek Revival style in the early 20th century, while the adjoining 1988 concrete-and-glass addition boosts the building's size and spirits. The next building is **State Parliament House**, an elegantly colonnaded building that has resounded with political debates (and much invective, not all of it sober), since 1827 (Parliament is open to the public weekdays 9am–5pm; free tours available Mon and Fri and daily during school holidays 1.30pm; bookings required tel: 02 9230-3444).

Sydney Hospital superseded the Rum Hospital of the early colonial days (see page 18). Built in the 1880s, it is the oldest hospital in Australia. Outside stands a bronze statue of **Il Porcellino**, a wild boar, a replica of a 17th-century original in Florence. The statue was donated by an Italian immigrant whose relatives had worked at the hospital. Patting its snout is said to bring good luck. Tours highlighting the history and architecture of the hospital are offered daily. There is a charge, and booking is required (tel: 02 9382-7111).

The **Mint** (tel: 02 8239-2288; Mon–Fri 9.30am–5pm) next door, originally the Rum Hospital's south wing, was converted into a mint to process gold-rush bullion midway through the 19th century. In the early days it was used to produce 'holey dollars' – Spanish coins recycled to ease a desperate shortage of cash. It ceased operating as a mint in 1926, and now houses a small display on the site's history.

Immediately opposite, a huge brown block-like building houses the **State and Commonwealth Law Courts**. This modern contribution to Macquarie Street, out of scale with the opposite side of the street, is adorned with Australia's coat of arms – an emu and kangaroo each trying to look fierce. The forecourt is enlivened at times by the arrival of barristers in gowns and wigs.

Hyde Park Barracks ⓬ (tel: 02 8239-2311; daily 10am–5pm), next to the Mint, was commissioned by Governor Macquarie to house 600 male convicts. It was designed by Francis Greenway, pardoned forger and architectural genius. Completed in 1819 and adorned with a fine colonial clock, this is perhaps the best Georgian building in Sydney. At various times it housed 'unprotected females' and Irish orphans.

The barracks is now a museum of Sydney's early days, with an emphasis on giving an insight into the lives of convicts. A convict dormitory with hammocks has been reconstructed on the third floor. A computer base gives public access to the records of every prisoner

War mementoes

Pine trees around Hyde Park's Anzac War Memorial were grown from seeds gathered at Gallipoli in Turkey, where soldiers from the Australian and New Zealand Corps (Anzac) fought in 1915.

who passed through the institution. The museum also features displays of photographs, pictures, letters and objects dating from the convict period.

Anzac War Memorial

Hyde Park ⑬, at the end of Macquarie Street, is a fraction the size of its London namesake, but it provides the same green relief. The land was cleared at the beginning of the 19th century, with a racetrack being its first big attraction. Hyde Park was the venue for boxing matches, and was also the new colony's first cricket pitch. The two most formal features of these 16-hectare (40-acre) gardens are the **Anzac War Memorial** ⑭, commemorating the country's war dead, and the **Archibald Fountain**, an extravaganza of statuary on mythical themes, with a fine plume of water.

Sightseers who enjoy old places of worship should mark three targets on the edge of Hyde Park. To the north, the early colonial **St James's Church** on Queen's Square was designed by Francis Greenway as a courthouse and consecrated in 1824. When its use was changed, the intended cells were converted into a crypt. Across College Street to the east, twin-spired **St Mary's Cathedral** stands on the site of the colony's first Catholic church, and from the same era, the magnificent **Great Synagogue** faces the park from the opposite side, across Elizabeth Street.

The **Australian Museum** ⑮ (www.australianmuseum.net.au; daily 9.30am–5pm except Christmas Day) at 6 College Street was established in 1827. It is a contemporary hub of information, education, resources and research, with an expanding collection of over 18 million items. Public areas include Surviving Australia, which reveals how Australia's unique animals have evolved in harsh environments, Indigenous Australians, which looks at the culture and history of Aboriginal and Torres Strait Islander people, and it has exhibits on dinosaurs, skeletons and an extensive minerals display which includes gold, diamonds and Australian opal.

DARLING HARBOUR

Darling Harbour ⑯, a vast tourist and leisure centre, offers parks, a light and airy shopping complex, the Convention and Exhibition Centre, restaurants and museums.

Despite its proximity to Sydney's centre, Darling Harbour has never been fully integrated with the central city. It lies alongside the CBD like an island. The **Monorail**, closed in 2013, used to link the CBD with Darling Harbour's diverse elements. Nowadays, you can take the train to Town Hall station and walk along Bathurst Street to the new Darling Quarter or access the Harbour by Light Rail.

To reach Darling Harbour from the city, you are probably better off walking across Pyrmont Bridge, which runs off the end of Market Street. The 1902 bridge is constructed of wood and was the first electrically operated swing-span bridge in the world. It was designed by Percy Allan who was renowned for his common sense approach to engineering, which was characterised by an economical use of materials, easy construction and keeping up with general maintenance. The bridge is generally opened for demonstrations on weekends and public holidays.

Historic Pyrmont Bridge

WHERE TO EAT AND SHOP

On the western side of Darling Harbour, Harbourside Shopping Centre offers more than 200 shops and boutiques with an emphasis on Australia-made merchandise. There's a fresh-food precinct and a large food court. An entertainment level includes such diversions as a bowling centre and a Boeing 737-800 flight simulator. Dining options range from cheap and cheerful snacks to stylish restaurants serving cuisine from around the world. Most places overlook the water.

On the eastern side of Darling Harbour is the upmarket development **Cockle Bay Wharf**. You can enjoy food from the Adriatic Sea coasts at Adria, Mod Oz cuisine and exotic cocktails at Blackbird, and a decadent selection of desserts at Lindt Chocolat Café. Nick's 103 serves breakfast by the waterfront.

On the north side of Pyrmont Bridge is the ferry wharf and Sydney Aquarium (see page 53), beyond which is **King Street**

Wharf, another dining and nightclub area. Eateries here range from the affordable Kobe Jones which serves delicious Japanese dishes and Malaya (the place to try Laska and Rendang) to the Mediterranean ambiance of George's; you can do a lot worse than spend an evening working your way through its mezze menu with a good friend and a bottle of wine.

MAIN ATTRACTIONS

Next to Harbourside Shopping Centre, the **Australian National Maritime Museum ⑰** (www.anmm.gov.au; daily 9.30am–5pm) attracts more than 120,000 international visitors a year. Housed in a large white building with a wave-form roof, the museum displays more than 2,000 maritime objects in permanent and temporary exhibitions. Moored at wharves outside is

The Chinese Garden

the museum's fleet of 14 historic vessels, including a submarine and a replica of Cook's ship, the *Endeavour*.

The area is currently undergoing a significant redevelopment with the newest additions including the International Convention Centre, housing a theatre and a luxury hotel as well as conference rooms, and The Ribbon tower, an architectural marvel that will house the new IMAX theatre among other things.

At the southern tip of the water is **Tumbalong Park** offers open spaces, brilliantly original fountains, geometrical challenges, swings, slides and mazes.

Right in the heart of the Darling Harbour is the **Pumphouse**, a former hydraulic power station, now a tavern featuring 60 beers from across Australia and the rest of the world. It's well worth the short walk to the **Powerhouse Museum** on Harris Street

(www.maas.museum/powerhouse-museum; daily 10am–5pm), which focuses on science and design. Its hands-on exhibits are popular with children.

Darling Harbour's **Chinese Garden** ⓲ (daily 9.30am–5.30pm) was a joint effort by the governments of New South Wales and the Chinese province of Guangdong. This 1-hectare (2.5-acre) garden allows quiet contemplation amid apricot, azalea, jasmine and weeping willow trees overhanging paths, ponds and rock formations. **Sea Life Sydney Aquarium** ⓳ (www.sydneyaquarium.com.au; daily 9.30am–7pm), on the city side of Darling Harbour, is one of the largest aquariums in the world, and one of the city's biggest attractions. There are over 13,000 animals from over 700 different species here, including fish, sharks, crocodiles, turtles, eels, jellyfish, seals, penguins and platypus. Three oceanariums with tunnels allow you to stroll under the water while the denizens of the deep swim above, below and beside you. The aquarium is home to two of the only six dugongs on display in the world and one of the largest collections of sharks. The Great Barrier Reef exhibit is the largest in the world and includes one of the oceanariums, live coral caves, a coral atoll and a tropical touch-pool; in total, the complex houses over 6,000 animals from the Great Barrier Reef.

Adjacent to the aquarium is **Sydney Wildlife World** (www.wildlifesydney.com.au; daily 10am–5pm). This enclosed mini-zoo features 65 interactive displays and walk-through habitats of 130 species of Australian fauna from all parts of the continent, including spiders, snakes, lizards, parrots, cassowary, wallabies and wombats. The star attractions, however, are the koalas. You can have your photo taken with one (at extra cost). Purchase a joint ticket and you can visit Wildlife World and the aquarium.

EASTERN SUBURBS

KINGS CROSS

Bright lights and shady characters exist side by side in **Kings Cross ⑳**, a couple of railway stops from Circular Quay. 'The Cross', as it's often called, is a bit sleazy, crawling with hedonists and counter-culturalists of all persuasions and in the 80's and 90's the motto was 'if it's excessive, it's here'.

The Cross's main drag is **Darlinghurst Road**; it's still dotted with a jumble of bars, strip joints, fast-food outlets, tattoo parlours and X-rated shops but change is in the air, as gentrification sets in. Buildings which once housed notorious clubs have been sold and have been turned into sleek apartments and residential housing following strict noise curfews passed in 2014. A number of trendy bars, cool nightclubs and boutique hotels have opened. Even the Bourbon and Beefsteak Bar, which was once a gloriously tacky icon of the Cross, has been given a slick revamp and a change of name to The Bourbon.

In the evenings, you're likely to encounter prostitutes plying their trade from doorways in the Cross. Prostitution is legal in Sydney, provided streetwalkers observe rules such as staying away from schools, churches and private homes. The Cross has a thriving drugs trade, which has survived all attempts to eradicate it, but you probably won't be offered drugs unless you seek them. Visitors should use caution in this area, especially at night, as muggings do occur, and the hawkers outside strip bars and nightclubs can sometimes be intimidating.

A 5-minute walk from Kings Cross train station, on Onslow Avenue, **Elizabeth Bay House** is a magnificent home built between 1835 and 1839

Old house in Kings Cross

The beautiful staircase at Elizabeth Bay House

for the Colonial Secretary. Built in the style of a Grecian villa, it is a reminder that Kings Cross was a fashionable address for at least a century. It is open for tours during weekends. In the years after World War II, wealthier residents departed and less reputable elements moved in. Many of the former grand homes in the Cross were converted to boarding houses or backpacker lodgings.

Victoria Street, which runs off Darlinghurst Road, is a complete contrast to the main strip. It's lined with gracious old homes, trendy cafés, such as Infinity Sourdough Bakery, and fine restaurants, such as Mercato e Cucina and A Tavola. In the 1970s, Victoria Street became a battleground, with residents and unions pitted against rapacious property developers – the latter seeking to demolish homes to build high-rises. Juanita Nielsen, a celebrated Sydney heiress who edited a newspaper called *Now*, was a valiant campaigner for preservation. Although her efforts helped avert much high-rise ugliness, Ms Nielsen roused the ire of unscrupulous developers. She disappeared in July 1975 and was never seen again.

Also worth a look is Macleay Street, which runs through the upmarket residential area of **Potts Point**. Art Deco apartment buildings jostle with cafés, restaurants, bookshops, delis and art galleries, and there are occasional glimpses of the harbour.

PADDINGTON

Another inner-city suburb worth investigating is **Paddington ㉑**, to the southeast of Kings Cross. Intricate wrought-ironwork, commonly known as Sydney Lace, is the local trademark; it adorns the balconies of many 19th-century terraced houses. Paddington was developed for workers' housing in the 1880s, but fell into dilapidation and by the 1940s had become a slum. A slow process of gentrification then began, and by the 1970s 'Paddo', as the locals affectionately call it, had become a fashionable, rather artsy place to live.

The suburb is now fully gentrified, with residents more likely to be lawyers or stockbrokers than artists. The adjoining suburb of Woollahra, studded with mansions and consulates, is even more leafy and patrician, with an excellent set of shops down Queen Street and Jersey Road.

Paddington offers plenty of ethnic restaurants, antiques shops, art galleries, fashionable bookshops and trendy boutiques. One of Sydney's best public markets, Paddington Markets, is held each Saturday at 395 Oxford Street on the grounds of Paddington Uniting Church. It features over 200 stalls of mostly high-end merchandise.

Great shopping and dining are found along **Oxford Street** and the nearby intersection called **Five Ways**. The section of

Oxford Street running through the suburb of Darlinghurst is a centre for Sydney's large gay community. The Oxford Hotel (134 Oxford Street) is the street's longest-established gay pub, and there are many more bars and nightclubs.

Victoria Barracks, built by convicts in the 1840s to house a regiment of British soldiers and their families, covers almost 12 hectares (30 acres). It is still an active military centre. A former gaol houses a museum of Australia's military heritage (tours offered Thu between 10am and 1pm and Sun between 10am–3pm, by appointment; tel: 02 9339-3330 for reservations).

CENTENNIAL PARK

In 1811, the far-sighted Governor Macquarie set aside an area outside the city for public use, naming it Sydney Common. The Governor's original 405-hectare (1,000-acre) bequest has been much whittled away since, alas, but Centennial Park (at the eastern end of Oxford Street, south of Woollahra) is a welcome remnant.

The park's 189 hectares (467 acres) of trees, lawns, duck ponds, rose gardens, bridle paths and sports fields are visited by about 3 million people a year, who cycle, rollerblade, walk their dogs, feed birds, fly kites, picnic and barbecue.

Centennial Park is a popular venue for birdwatchers and nature-lovers. Nearly 130 native land and water birds visit the park. Among the many distinctive species are long-beaked ibises, which look like something from the wall of an ancient Egyptian tomb but are native to Australia. Flocks of loud-squawking, sulphur-crested cockatoos regularly make their presence known. Bats twitter in the park's huge and venerable Moreton Bay fig trees, and native Australian possums, blue-tongued lizards and other creatures dwell among the native

Perusing goods at the market

trees and flowers. An extensive schedule of tours and activities is offered (tel: 02 9339-6699; www.centennialparklands.com. au). Bicycles and pedal-carts can be rented from Centennial Park Cycles (tel: 02 9398-5027; www.cyclehire.com.au).

Centennial Park Homestead (www.cenntenialhomestead. com.au) is a lovely setting for a light meal and a glass of wine (Wisteria Room) or an elegant dinner (Kitchen), while the Pantry has a menu of takeaway items for an impromptu picnic.

Centennial Park Amphitheatre provides an outdoor venue for events and productions. In the summer months, a popular Moonlight Cinema programme is held in the amphitheatre. Films start at about 8.30pm. It is popular, so it is a good idea to book beforehand (www.moonlight.com.au).

Adjoining Centennial Park, Moore Park houses the **Sydney Cricket Ground** (a landmark to cricket fans around the world; Aussie Rules football is played here in winter), **Sydney Football**

Sydney Cricket Ground

Stadium (for rugby league, rugby union and soccer; currently closed for redevelopment, due to reopen in 2020) and the **Equestrian Centre**. If you fancy a ride on the bridle path, contact with Papillon Riding Stables (tel: 02 8356 9866).

In a controversial move, 24 hectares (59 acres) of the park were handed over to media tycoon Rupert Murdoch's Fox Group, for redevelopment into a studio and entertainment complex. The **Entertainment Quarter** (formerly Fox Studios) has shops, bars, restaurants and cafés, an indoor children's playground, thrill rides, a 12-screen cinema complex and venues for live entertainment, such as the Comedy Store. A farmers' market takes place here every Wednesday and Saturday (8am–2pm), with a vegan market taking over every third Sunday of the month (9am–5pm).

INNER WEST SUBURBS

NEWTOWN
Newtown ㉒, in Sydney's Inner West, 4km (21.5 miles) from the CBD, is perhaps Sydney's most lively neighbourhood. Its cosmopolitan nature and its high proportion of students

(many attending the University of Sydney, just down the road) give the suburb a raffish flavour. Originally, Newtown consisted of farms on the outskirts of Sydney. Wealthy merchants built villas here in the early 1800s, but the late 19th century brought industry and workers' cottages and terraces. By the 1970s, Newtown had become a cheap-rent suburb. Renewal has meant the renovation of many of the classic Victorian-era buildings as well as the transformation of warehouses, commercial sites, even storage silos into smart flats and housing units.

Today, it is known for the broad demographics of its population: students, young professionals, artists, gays, shopkeepers, New Age traders and young families also share the district. Over a third of the residents were born somewhere other than Australia. It's a tolerant, accepting neighbourhood in a city already known for its diversity. Look for the community festivals celebrating the ethnic and cultural diversity of the area throughout the year.

The main thoroughfare is King Street, which is a lively and entertaining quarter with over 600 shopfront delis, cafés, retro-fashion outlets, pubs, stores selling yoga accessories and eco-friendly toys and independent bookstores – there is even a shop selling nothing but buttons. It is sometimes called 'eat street' because of the large number of restaurants located here, many of which are very small outlets selling 'home cooking' from around the globe.

The northern end of King Street has moved upmarket, but the diversity and smaller businesses are still found in the central and, increasingly, southern end of the street. This end of the street also takes on a Pacific Island flavour at weekends, when Sydney's Polynesian and Melanesian population head there to shop for Pacific Island spices and produce.

Newtown has some great pubs and bars. The Courthouse Hotel at 202 Australia Street can be noisy and crowded in the main bar, but its huge beer garden, under frangipani trees with the massive barbie, gets good reviews. The family-owned Bank Hotel at 324 King Street is also a nice place for libations; three bars on different levels cater to all moods – from mellow jazz on the deck at sunset to late-night jamming DJs.

BALMAIN

Balmain ㉓, which is close to the CBD and easily accessible by ferry (from Wharf 5 at Circular Quay to Darling Street Wharf) and by bus (from the QVB or Central Station), is located on a peninsula and retains a sense of separateness from the city. A visit here by ferry, which sails beneath the Harbour Bridge, is strongly recommended.

Well into the latter half of the 20th century, Balmain was staunchly working-class. The suburb was settled by sailors and boatbuilders in the 1840s. It's become the abode of successful actors, lawyers, and others who can afford the steep property prices. Its village character survives, however.

Balmain's main road is Darling Street, where the historic, popular and pet-friendly London Hotel stands more or less opposite St Andrews Congregational Church. A lively flea market takes place around the church on Saturdays, with equal measures of stalls selling high-end accessories, vintage clothing, hand-crafted sterling silver jewellery and all sorts of food stalls (you'll find Egyptian, Indian, Lebanese and vegetarian, among others).

Darling Street has the most shops, although rising rents are forcing out many of the smaller, unique shops and seeing them replaced by chain stores. Stop at Victoire Boulangerie (660 Darling Street) for classic breads and pastries. At Bertoni Casalinga (281 Darling Street), Mama supervises the Italian

dishes that emerge from the kitchen. Jazz-lovers frequent Unity Hall Hotel (292 Darling Street) for Sunday afternoon jazz, while those who like fine food at affordable prices gravitate to Darlingreen (231 Darling Street). Sydney Ferries publishes a harbour walks guide which includes directions for a memorable walk from Darling Street Wharf, along part of Darling Street, and ending at Birchgrove Wharf. Louisa Road in Birchgrove is one of Sydney's top real-estate strips, with no shortage of millionaires' townhouses. There are great harbour views from Birchgrove Wharf.

LEICHHARDT

Although it is named after a Prussian explorer, **Leichhardt** ㉔ is home to Sydney's 'Little Italy'. Italian immigrants began settling here in the 19th century, and it soon became known for its Italian groceries and restaurants.

Today, less than 5 percent of Leichhardt's current population was born in Italy, but many residents of Italian extraction call it *'casa'*. Norton Street is the best place to browse; eateries include Jovanotti (20 Norton Street) for traditional Italian fare, At Fernando's (118 Norton Street) for original Italian meals, and La Botte D'Oro, a trattoria at 137 Marion Street.

WESTERN SUBURBS

Sydney's western suburbs stretch for many kilometres, almost to the foot of the Blue Mountains. This is where most Sydneysiders live. Visitors can safely ignore the majority of it.

Waterfront mansions on the Parramatta River

PARRAMATTA

Parramatta, on the Parramatta River, is almost as old as Sydney. In the 1790s, many of Sydney's administrative functions and all its farming efforts were moved upriver to Parramatta, where the soil was more fertile. Governor Phillip said he would have founded the colony on this spot if he had known about it earlier. In 1804, a group of 260 Irish convicts led a rebellion at Parramatta aimed at overthrowing the Governor, but troops crushed the uprising. Most of the conspirators were hanged.

Many Parramatta buildings are new and not particularly inspiring, but a few places of interest remain, including Elizabeth Farm, Old Government House in Parramatta Park, and Experiment Farm cottage. For the most pleasant and most scenic hour-long ride to Parramatta, catch one of the RiverCat catamaran ferries at Circular Quay.

SYDNEY OLYMPIC PARK

The Olympic Games last just two weeks but their effects linger. In Sydney's case, the 2000 Olympics created huge new parks and state-of-the-art sports facilities.

The fastest way to get to **Sydney Olympic Park** in the suburb of Homebush is to take a train from Central Station to Olympic Park station. A more scenic alternative is to climb aboard a RiverCat catamaran at Circular Quay and cruise up the Parramatta River to Sydney Olympic Park wharf. The ride takes about an hour. The visitor centre (tel: 02 9714-7888; www.sydneyolympicpark.com.au) has details of the range of tours available. You can pick up a map and do a self-guided tour. Alternatively, an hour-long guided walking tour, the Games Trail, visits the various sporting facilities, including the observation deck of the Novotel Olympic Park, which gives panoramic views of the Olympic site, the Blue Mountains, the Harbour Bridge and the city's skyscrapers. Other tours are conducted via narrow-gauge rail, trams and Segway. There is a separate 70-minute tour of just the stadium, during which you can have your photo taken on an Olympic medal dais. You can hire a bike to explore over 35km (22 miles) of trails which surround Sydney Olympic Park.

FEATHERDALE WILDLIFE PARK

Those interested in getting close to normally shy Australian wildlife should make the trip to **Featherdale Wildlife Park** (tel: 02 9622-1644; www.featherdale.com.au; daily 9am–5pm) in the suburb of Doonside, about an hour's drive from the CBD. With over 300 species of Australian wildlife, you can feed the kangaroos and wallabies, have your photo taken with a koala, watch the crocodiles being fed, or just wander around admiring the other animal inmates, including wombats, emus, dingoes, Tasmanian devils, snakes and a variety of birdlife. The park can be reached by taking a train from the city to Blacktown and then a bus to the

⊘ VIP FROGS RULE

The rare green-and-golden bell frog, a threatened species, makes its home in a disused brick pit on part of the Sydney Olympic Park site. This reclusive little amphibian happens to bear Australia's sporting colours. Under the original Olympic site plan, the frog's home was to have given way to the Olympic Tennis Centre. But the 300 or so frogs refused to move, even when a new pond was built for them. As a result, the Tennis Centre was moved and the brick pit was incorporated into the area's parklands. The brick-pit is now used to store water for the Olympic site's recycled water system – a compromise that won't harm the frogs.

park entrance; some bus tours also stop at the park on their way to the Blue Mountains. The park is a past winner of a New South Wales tourism award.

THE BEACHES

Sydney has dozens of beaches, offering everything from raging surf to lapping waves. At ocean beaches heed the advice to swim only between the red-and-yellow flags, which

Bondi is Sydney's most popular beach

indicate sections of beach patrolled by professional lifeguards or volunteer lifesavers. Strong currents and tidal rips are a feature of many Sydney beaches; drownings are an unfortunate part of every summer – many victims are tourists who swim outside the flags or are unused to swimming in strong surf. Drowning between the flags, however, is virtually unheard of.

BONDI BEACH

Pronounced 'bond-eye', Australia's most famous stretch of sand is central Sydney's nearest beach, easily accessible by bus (number 380 or 333), from Circular Quay, which takes about 45 minutes, or by train to Bondi Junction, from where there are frequent buses to the beach. It's an 11-minute ride from Town Hall station.

Site of surf shops, cafés and lively alfresco restaurants, **Bondi** ㉕ has been popular ever since trams started running there

Bathers at Clovelly

in 1894. Its appeal has outlasted the trams. Style purists consider Bondi's appearance a bit tacky, but its fortunes are climbing and the suburb has become quite fashionable. Many Australian celebrities call Bondi home. Bondi Pavilion, which houses dressing rooms for 1,000 people, a grand ballroom and other vital beach facilities, displays photos of the beach dating back to the mid-19th century, when it was privately owned and utterly deserted.

Backpackers use Bondi to celebrate Christmas riotously and see in the New Year. Mainstream beach-users include lithe and leathery veteran sun-worshippers, fanatical surfers and families at play. Bondi is Sydney's most popular beach, and it can be crowded, especially at weekends.

The cliffs around Bondi's southern end offer a bracing walk and enchanting views, especially in the early evening by the light of a full moon. If you follow the walk south from Bondi, you will reach **Tamarama Beach**. Popular with the body-beautiful set, it is often called 'Glamarama Beach'. Next stop is **Bronte Beach**, backed by palms and pines. It has great facilities, including a sea pool for those who dislike strong surf, and a big park for picnicking. It's a favourite of families. Further along are **Clovelly Beach**, basically a very large and sheltered rock pool with good snorkelling, and then the much larger **Coogee Beach**. Popular with backpackers, it usually has gentle surf, making it good for swimming.

VAUCLUSE AND SOUTH HEAD

The peninsula jutting north from Bondi to Watsons Bay and culminating in South Head offers superlative beaches and great walks. Much of Sydney's most expensive residential real estate is located around here, in Vaucluse (just south of Watsons Bay), and in Point Piper (a peninsula to the west of Vaucluse, separated from it by the almost equally wealthy suburb of Rose Bay).

The Bondi Explorer bus (see page 131) allows you to travel on a scenic tour from Circular Quay. The ticket allows unlimited on-and-off access to 19 stops along the oceanfront (daily 8.45am–4.15pm). One loop of the route takes about 90 minutes. Alternatively, take the ferry from Circular Quay to Watsons Bay Wharf. Houses in the Vaucluse/Watsons Bay area are lavish but tasteful, with occasional exceptions to each of those criteria. The winding streets are bougainvillea-lined, and the surroundings have a secluded, villagey charm. All along the route you'll catch splendid views of the city.

Camp Cove at **Watsons Bay** is the spot where Governor Arthur Phillip first stepped ashore in Sydney Harbour (on 20 January 1788) after abandoning Botany Bay further south. The governor had taste – the beach at Camp Cove is one of Sydney's finest. A plaque notes where Phillip landed. For a short but very worthwhile excursion, take the stairs at the northern end of the beach (to your right as you face the harbour) and follow the path to South Head lighthouse, which stands on a headland overlooking the entrance to Sydney Harbour. The views of harbour and ocean are magnificent. Also at Watsons Bay is the very popular Doyles on the Beach, a near-legendary – and particularly expensive – seafood restaurant.

Vaucluse House ㉖, a stately home with its own beach in the pretty suburb of Vaucluse, adds its mock-Gothic turrets to Sydney's harbour skyline. The mansion began as the home of a colourful convict, Sir Henry Brown Hayes, the Sheriff of Cork before he was banished to Australia for the abduction of his bride. In the 1830s the new owner, William Wentworth, expanded it into a 15-bedroom homestead (grounds daily 10am–5pm; house Wed–Sun 10am–4pm; charge for house).

⊘ BEACH DRESS CODE

Dress on Sydney's beaches has come a long way over the past century. In the 1900s, the law permitted public swimming only in the early morning and after dark. This law was successfully challenged, and by the 1920s the beaches of Sydney were crowded with people, but they had to wear neck-to-knee bathing costumes. In 1935, an ordinance was passed forbidding men to wear swimming attire that exposed their chests. Beach inspectors were empowered to remove offenders to a dressing enclosure, where they could be compelled to clothe themselves 'respectably'. By the 1960s, regulations had mellowed considerably, although beach inspectors still prowled the sands searching for excessively brief costumes (the focus by that time had shifted to women). Sydney has three legally sanctioned nudist beaches: Lady Jane Bay, Cobblers Beach and Obelisk Beach.

You can also grab lunch and afternoon tea in the sunny courtyard daily (tel: 02 9388-8188).

Not far south of Watsons Bay (towards the city) is **Nielsen Park**, full of shady trees and one of Sydney's top spots for picnicking and swimming. It is part of Sydney Harbour National Park. Nielsen Park has its own excellent little bay – which is generally referred to as Nielsen Park Bay rather

Boats moored at Vaucluse Bay

than its real name, Shark Bay. The beach is shark-netted, so you needn't fear any risk of being nipped. The beach has been extensively refurbished in the past few years, including the beach house and café. The headland towards Vaucluse Point (to the right of the beach when you face the harbour) is often quite secluded, even on public holidays. To the left of the beach, a walking track takes you southwards along the harbour's edge almost to Rose Bay.

MANLY

Manly ㉗ is reached from Circular Quay via a 30-minute ferry ride or the 17-minute high-speed Manly Fast Ferry. Both dock at the renovated Manly Wharf, a food, entertainment and activities centre. As Sydney's first seaside resort, it offers everything from beachfront dining and art galleries to parasailing and surfing schools. Manly offers a choice of two beaches – one open to the ocean and popular with surfers, the other a calm harbourside crescent suitable for children – and excellent views of Sydney Harbour. The area was named by Governor Phillip, who thought the Aborigines sunning themselves on the beach had a commanding ('manly') presence.

Linking the two beaches, the Corso is a promenade lined with shops, cafés, restaurants and fast-food emporia; fish 'n' chips is a speciality. Manly maintains a holiday atmosphere and has for decades used the slogan, 'Seven miles from Sydney and a thousand miles from care.'

The oceanside beach, divided into North Steyne and South Steyne, is lined with Norfolk pines and pleasant cafés. If you walk south (to the right as you face the ocean) along South Steyne, you end up at Shelly Beach Park, with

Manly has a relaxed holiday atmosphere

a sheltered little beach perfect for children. The park is a romantic place at sunset, when the sky turns red and gold.

A path runs from Manly to the Spit Bridge, a distance of almost 10km (6 miles), or 4 hours' walking time. The route stays close to the harbour all the way, and features bush land, beaches and bays, as well as harbour views. There are opportunities for you to have a swim and to fuel up on refreshments along the way, and at Grotto Point there are Aboriginal rock carvings.

A lifeguard takes to the surf

NORTHERN BEACHES

North of Manly, a couple of Pacific beaches with charming names, **Curl Curl** and **Dee Why**, offer good surfing. **Collaroy** and **Narrabeen** are linked by a single beach with an ocean pool, ideal for families. **Newport Beach** is a beautiful, broad sweep of sand. **Avalon Beach** is known for surfing and popular with children. **Whale Beach** is another good surfing beach with a wonderfully relaxed feel to it. At the northern tip of the Sydney beach region, **Palm Beach** – the abode of millionaires, actors and advertising types – is in a class of its own. Manicured, nicely gardened villas occupy the hills of the peninsula. If you're feeling like a climb, you can walk to the top of Barrenjoey Point at the beach's northern end. From the base of the lighthouse there are fantastic views over the mouth of Broken Bay – which marks Sydney's northern boundary. Tours of the lighthouse are offered on Sundays, weather permitting (tel: 02 9472-9300).

EXCURSIONS FROM SYDNEY

Within striking distance of Sydney – by car, train or sightseeing coach – a choice of scene-changers shows the wide variety of attractions on offer in New South Wales. Any of the more popular outings will deepen your understanding of Australia and its assets.

BLUE MOUNTAINS

Undeveloped native forest protected within national parks surrounds Sydney on three sides. The most popular destination – 1.5 hours' drive or a 2-hour rail trip west of the city – is **Blue Mountains National Park 28**, one of the most spectacular and captivating wilderness areas in Australia and a World Heritage listed region. The mountains really do look blue, given the right conditions: the blue tint is created by the refraction of light through the haze of volatile eucalyptus oil evaporating from the trees.

You can sign up for one of the many day tours from Sydney, or you can visit and explore at your own pace (Blue Mountain Visitors Centre, tel: 1300 653 408). Don't expect sharp peaks such as those in the Swiss Alps or Wyoming's Grand Tetons – the range is far too ancient and eroded for that. Here immense bush-filled canyons and ravines, weathered precipices, deep river valleys and soaring sandstone cliffs awe the viewer. The main road through the mountains is the Great Western Highway, which climbs through a succession of towns with the forest yawning

below and lines of hills gradually dissolving into the pale-blue eucalyptus haze.

Rising to a height of more than 1,300m (4,260ft), the Blue Mountains offer crisp air, vast sandstone valleys where waterfalls shatter on the rocks, gardens that burn with autumn colour, English-style homesteads and little towns of wood and stone. It is one of the few places in Australia where it gets cold enough to snow occasionally in midwinter, usually around August. At that time, one of the Blue Mountains' most photographed formations, the **Three Sisters**, is sometimes dusted with snow. Towns stage 'Yulefests' in July – winter in Australia – complete with Santa Claus and traditional Christmas fare. Historic towns like Katoomba, Blackheath, Wentworth Falls, Leura and Mount Victoria each boast gardens, any manner of accommodation and fabulous vistas. In the tiny hamlet of

Medlow Bath, the Art Deco Hydro Majestic Hotel, built as a European-style spa in the 1930s, is well worth a visit.

The Blue Mountains' largest town, **Katoomba**, is the usual starting point for most visitors. Nearby **Echo Point** has great viewing platforms that provide breathtaking views of the national park's forested valleys and near-vertical sandstone cliffs. A number of walking tracks also start from here – they are suitable for walkers of all fitness levels; information on them is available from Echo Point's visitor information centre.

If you have the energy, descend the Giant Stairway and walk down into the Jamison Valley, then take the **Scenic Railway** (charge) back up. The railway is a 3-minute hair-raising ride along an old mining cart track with the steepest incline in the world. The clifftop railway terminus is at **Scenic World** (tel: 02 4780-0200 or

Scenic Skyway

1300-SKYWAY; www.scenic world.com.au; daily 9am–5pm; charge for excursions and rides), a tourist complex a short distance to the west of Echo Point. Scenic World also offers the **Scenic Cableway**, which descends over 500m (1,600ft) into the Jamison Valley, the **Scenic Skyway**, a cable car dangling high above the valley and the **Scenic Walkway**, a boardwalk through the rainforest.

Jurassic plant

The Wollemi pine, the world's oldest species of tree, was discovered in a remote part of the Blue Mountains in 1994. The tree's closest relations became extinct during the Jurassic and Cretaceous periods – 200–65 million years ago. As one Sydney-based botanist exclaimed at the time, 'This is like finding a living dinosaur in your backyard.'

If you have time to spare, take a trip to a less touristed lookout, **Govetts Leap**, near Blackheath, 12km (7.5 miles) west of Katoomba. The views are perhaps even more spectacular, while the comparative lack of crowds gives a better sense of the wilderness around you.

The Aboriginal Blue Mountain Walkabout Tour gives a unique perspective into the connection between Australia's indigenous people and their land. The tour is conducted by Evan Yanna Muru, an Aborigine born on Darug land, and is a one-day immersion course in Aboriginal culture taught with an interesting walkabout through often rugged bush (tel: 0408 443 822; www.bluemoun tainswalkabout.com; daily; reservations required).

JENOLAN CAVES

Further along the Great Western Highway, about 60km (38 miles) from Mount Victoria, is Australia's most famous underground attraction. Explorers have yet to penetrate the entire labyrinth of Jenolan Caves, but thousands have

admired the stalactites and stalagmites, underground rivers and other wonders of the 11 caves open to the public. There is a packed schedule of guided, self-guided and adventure tours on offer (tel: 02 6359-3911 or 1300-763-311; daily; times and prices vary by tour).

HUNTER VALLEY

The best-known wine-growing region in New South Wales is the **Hunter Valley** ㉙, a 2-hour drive north of Sydney. You can visit it as a day trip, but it's also a very popular destination for weekenders. It is possible to drive there independently, but if you want to indulge in any serious wine tasting, a better option is to join an organised wine-tasting tour from Sydney. There are several motor coach tours which visit the better-known vineyards. These generally include an escorted walking tour of the wine-making facilities and lots of time in the tasting rooms. A more personal tour is conducted by Richard Everett, a 30-year veteran of Australia's wine industry. Drawing on his experience and ties with wineries (many of which are not normally open to the public), he takes small groups of no more than eight, for a very personal tour (tel: 02 9484-0477; www.winecountrytours.com.au; daily by reservation).

Wine making is nothing new to this region. Vines from France and Spain were transplanted here early in the life of the colony, and by the mid-19th century the region was producing hundreds of thousands of bottles of wine a year. More recent refinements to the production process have resulted in a number of high-quality vintages.

The towns of **Cessnock** and **Pokolbin** are the main centres of the Lower Hunter Valley wine region. The visitor centre at Pokolbin supplies maps and brochures (tel: 02 4990-0900; www.winecountry.com.au; Mon–Sat 9am–5pm, Sun 9am–4pm). The Hunter's 130 wineries harvest their grapes in February and March, but they welcome visitors throughout the year. With neat, rolling vineyards, the Lower Hunter is one of Australia's most attractive wine-producing regions.

Most of the Hunter wineries are open for tastings. Major wineries include Tyrell's Wines, Lindemans Winery, Hungerford Hill, the Rosemount Estate, Rothbury Estate and the McWilliams Estate. The wines made by big-name producers shouldn't lull you into neglecting 'boutique' wines, many of which can be obtained only by buying a bottle from the person who tended the vines, picked the grapes and fretted over fermentation. Quite a few of these exclusive wineries are members of co-ops in Pokolbin. Look for the Small Winemakers Centre, Boutique Wine Centre and Hermitage Road Cellars.

When not in the vineyards, visitors to the Hunter Valley can amuse themselves with horse riding, bushwalking, golf, tennis, water sports and hot-air ballooning. Also try a picnic on a horse-drawn carriage or a bicycle trip along the vine trail.

HAWKESBURY RIVER

The Hawkesbury River winds for 480km (about 300 miles) on its way to the Pacific at Broken Bay, just beyond Palm Beach in the most northerly section of Greater Sydney. The Hawkesbury's gentle waters and ever-changing vistas – coves and bays and steep wooded banks – delight visitors. There are many places where you can hire a boat – Brooklyn, an hour's drive from Sydney, is one, as is Akuna Bay in Ku-ring-gai Chase National Park (a 40-minute drive from Sydney). Try, for example, Holidays Afloat (tel: 02 9985-5555; www.holidaysafloat.com.au) at Brooklyn, which rents out houseboats that sleep from two to ten people, or All Points Boating (tel: 0411-802-959; www.allpointsboating.com.au) with inflatable boats. You don't need a licence or any boating experience.

Ku-ring-gai Chase National Park covers 15,000 hectares (37,000 acres) of bush land fringing the Hawkesbury. If boating doesn't appeal, there are a number of scenic walks in the park, some leading down to secluded coves and beaches where, on weekdays, you may well be the only visitor. The Resolute Track leads to Aboriginal rock-art sites. West Head, within the park, has panoramic views of the Hawkesbury, Broken Bay, Pittwater (a bay to the west of Palm Beach) and the coast to the north. Park information is available from the Bobbin Head Visitor Centre (tel: 02 9472-8949).

The Hawkesbury area might have become Australia's national capital. In 1899, an extraordinary, utopian plan arose to build an Australian capital on the Hawkesbury headlands. To be called Pacivica, the city would have included buildings

A misty morning in the Southern Highlands

modelled on the Tower of London, Windsor Castle and other architectural icons of the empire. As you cruise these secluded waterways, you'll be delighted the plan was set aside.

SOUTHERN HIGHLANDS

Lush grazing land and orchards dotted with historic towns and villages lie to the southwest of Sydney. Towns worth visiting include **Mittagong** and **Bowral**, a picturesque town that holds a tulip festival every October. **Berrima** is a Georgian gem so well preserved the whole town is listed as a national monument. There are plenty of antiques shops, arts and crafts galleries and atmospheric tearooms. Among the most distinguished monuments, the Surveyor General Inn, established in 1834, claims to be Australia's oldest continuously licensed inn. Another landmark, Berrima Gaol, was built in the 1830s by those who were soon to inhabit it.

CANBERRA

Australia's custom-built national capital lies about 300km (185 miles) southwest of Sydney at the heart of the Australian Capital Territory, a 240-sq-km (93-sq-mile) expanse of farmland, mountains, forests and valleys. If you plan a day trip to **Canberra** ㉚ from Sydney, it is best to fly. Flights are frequent and take just 40 minutes. Buses make daily trips, but last over 3 hours each way. There are also three trains a day from Sydney.

Canberra is a quiet city, but it does have some of Australia's finest galleries and public buildings, and perhaps the loveliest surroundings of any national capital.

Created in 1901 when Australia decided it needed an independent capital free from political or commercial domination

Parliament House

by any one state, Canberra was designed by the Chicago landscape architect Walter Burley Griffin. A planned community created straight from the blueprints, Canberra has no old quarter and few restored historic buildings. The city's most prominent structure, **Parliament House** (tel: 02-6277-7111; daily 9am–5pm; guided tours at 9.30am, 11am, 1pm, 2pm and 3.30pm)

Seeing Canberra

Canberra is deceptively large, which can make it a challenge if you don't drive. A good option is the Explorer Bus. An all-day ticket provides a hop-on, hop-off service at all major and a few of the lesser-known attractions via a continuous loop with commentary about the sights. The bus picks up at several hotels.

on Capital Hill, opened in 1988. It replaced an earlier building from 1927, which now houses the **Museum of Australian Democracy** (tel: 02 6270-8222; daily 9am–5pm). Other attractions include the Australian National University, the National Film and Sound Archives, the Australian Institute of Sport, the National Museum of Australia, the National Portrait Gallery, the National Arboretum and the National Science and Technology Centre. There are also over 30 art and cultural institutions, ranging from Questacon at the National Science and Technology Centre which is fun for kids (tel: 02 6270-2800; daily 9am–5pm) to the **National Gallery of Australia** (tel: 02 6240-6411; www.nga.gov.au; daily 10am–5pm; free, except for some special exhibits), which houses the most extensive collection in Australia. Another major cultural institution, the **Australian War Memorial** (www.awm.gov.au; daily 10am–5pm), is devoted to Australian military history. The capital's other diversions include clubs, music venues and restaurants.

The historic Strand Arcade

 **WHAT TO DO**

SHOPPING

Sydney shopping hours generally run from 9am to 5.30pm Monday to Friday, 9am to 5pm on Saturday and 9am to 4pm on Sunday. Shops do not close for lunch. Thursday is late-night shopping in the Central Business District (CBD), when many stores stay open until 9pm. Other suburban centres have late-night shopping on other nights. Some shops at Darling Harbour and The Rocks stay open until 9pm daily.

Acceptance of American Express, Visa and MasterCard credit cards is virtually universal in Sydney, with lesser-known cards accepted at larger enterprises. International travellers can buy goods duty-free by producing their ticket and passport at the duty-free store when making a purchase. On departure the goods must be shown to the customs agent, who is tipped off by a computer system. (For further information on duty-free allowances, see page 133 or visit www.sydneyairport.com.au/prepare/departure.)

WHERE TO SHOP

In central Sydney, skyscrapers sit above subterranean shopping arcades. **Pitt Street Mall** is a pedestrian-only street linked to several shopping plazas. For shopping in a historic atmosphere, try the **Queen Victoria Building (QVB)** on George Street, or the stylish **Strand Arcade**, a

Tax refunds

Australia operates a Tourist Refund Scheme under which overseas visitors can claim a refund of the Goods and Services Tax (GST) added to most purchases. For more information see www.abf.gov.au/entering-and-leaving-Australia.

Victorian masterpiece running between George and Pitt streets. Some of Australia's leading fashion designers have boutiques on the upper levels of the Strand. It's also worth inspecting the jewellery shops. Other shopping locations include the **Imperial Arcade**, running between Pitt and Castlereagh streets, the adjacent **Skygarden** and **Centrepoint**, **Glasshouse** on King Street and **Galeries Victoria** on George Street opposite the QVB. Go to Darlinghurst, Paddington or Woollahra for local jewellery and fashion designers. Sydney's main department stores are David Jones (on Market Street) and Myer (on Pitt Street Mall). Many neighbourhoods host open-air markets at weekends. The Rocks Markets is known for its food stalls on Friday and higher-end clothing and art on Saturday and Sunday; Paddington, Balmain, Bondi Beach and Newtown are all known for their markets.

WHAT TO BUY

Aboriginal art. Aboriginal artists sell their work in art centres, specialist galleries and craft retailers, and through agents. Each artist owns the rights to his or her particular stories, motifs and totems. Galleries with reputations for quality original works include The Outback Centre in Darling Harbour, Coo-ee Aboriginal Art at Bondi Beach, Kate Owen's Gallery in Rozelle, Gannon House in The Rocks and Artery Contemporary Aboriginal Art in Darlinghurst.

Avoiding fakes

Fakes and kitsch are sometimes represented as Aboriginal art by unscrupulous traders. To help identify genuine Aboriginal and Torres Strait Islander art, Aboriginal communities have developed the Label of Authenticity, which employs the Aboriginal colours black, red and yellow and is protected by law.

Authentic didgeridoos

Antiques. The Paddington and Woollahra district is full of antiques shops. Worthy pieces to seek out include clocks, jewellery, porcelain, silverware, glassware, books and maps.

Fashion. Local labels include Country Road, Trent Nathan, Akira, Morrissey, Wayne Cooper, Scanlan & Theodore, Saba, and Marcs. For beachwear, look for Billabong and Mambo.

Outback clothing. A distinct style of clothing has evolved in Australia's rural bush. Driza-bone oilskin raincoats, Akubra hats and the R.M. Williams range of bushwear (including boots and moleskin trousers) are good examples. Blundstone boots, known for their durability, are another, and UGG boots are almost an Australian obsession. Australian merino sheep produce fine wool ideally suited for spinning.

Opals. Australia is the source of most of the world's opals. The different 'colours' determine the rarity and cost of the stone. 'Black' opals are the rarest and show streaks of colour in a dark stone; 'light' opals show swirls of colour on a white or light stone. 'Doublets' and 'triplets' are manufactured by gluing thin slices of opals to each other and to a backing to create a dramatic effect. While attractive, these are not highly valued. The Opal Association certifies dealers to ensure that they adhere to an ethical code of conduct.

Sapphires. After opals, sapphires are Australia's most mined gemstones. A sapphire is exactly the same stone as a ruby – the only difference is the name and the colour. Blue is the most common, but you'll find them in every colour of the rainbow. Shoppers should request a certificate of authenticity to confirm the quality of any stone or jewellery purchased.

Diamonds. Australia has one of the world's richest deposits of diamonds. The gems are mined by Argyle Diamond Mines in the Kimberley region in the west. Kimberley is famed for its 'pink' diamonds, sometimes marketed under the description 'champagne'. Make certain the hue of a coloured stone is natural – colours can be artificially created and enhanced.

SPORTS

Too much sport is barely enough. That's the way Sydneysiders feel about their weekends. If not actually playing or watching sport, they are reading about it, arguing about it, listening to it on the radio, watching it on TV or betting on it.

PARTICIPATORY SPORTS

Swimming and sunning. With dozens of alluring beaches and Olympic-size pools within easy reach, swimming is a major activity in Sydney. The more popular beaches are marked by yellow-and-red flags showing where it's safe to swim. Beware of strong undertows or shifting currents and obey the instructions of the lifeguards. If a shark alert is sounded (rare), beat a retreat to the shore. Other dangers are bluebottles, jellyfish-like creatures that inflict a painful (but non-fatal) sting. Blue-ringed octopuses are more dangerous but rare. At many beaches, you'll see a kiosk equipped with vinegar and other first-aid supplies for stings.

Surfing. Surfboard and bodyboard riders are not allowed within the swimming areas marked by yellow-and-red flags; 'surfcraft' areas are marked by signs. Many surf schools offer lessons in board-riding – try Let's Go Surfing at Bondi (tel: 02 9365-1800; www.letsgosurfing.com.au) or Manly Surf School (tel: 02 9932-7000; www.manlysurfschool.com). Surfing carnivals are among the highlights of the Sydney season from November to March.

Scuba-diving. North Head (near Manly) and Gordon's Bay (near Bondi) are favourite spots for scuba-divers. There are many other dive sites in New South Wales, though none is as spectacular as those of the Great Barrier Reef. In April 2011, the decommissioned frigate HMAS *Adelaide* was scuttled off the coast about an hour from Sydney. Divers are excited about the creation of this artificial reef. Professional diving schools offer classes

Catching a wave off Bondi

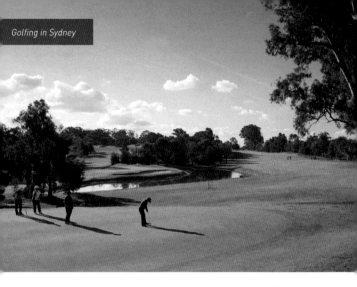

and dives for beginners and most advanced divers. Operators include Abyss, near Sydney (tel: 02 9583-9662; www.abyss.com.au), Manly Dive (tel: 02 9977-4355; www.divesydney.com.au) and Pro Dive with several locations including Coogee (tel: 02 8116-1199 or 1800 820 820; www.prodive.com.au).

Snorkelling. Snorkellers can walk from shore and enjoy watching fish, rays and the occasional octopus from the Sydney beaches. Popular locations are Clovelly and Gordon Bay.

Fishing. Offshore fishing is an ocean adventure. Try Deep Sea Charters (which uses a classic wooden trawler; tel: 0478-250-780; www.deepseacharters.com.au), Wahoo Charters (tel: 02 9687-2903; www.wahoocharters.info) or Bravo Fishing (tel: 02 9888-9494; www.bravofishing.com.au).

Sailing and boating. Sailing on Sydney Harbour is an unforgettable experience. Sydney by Sail probably has the most comprehensive services: 3-hour cruises around Sydney Harbour, charter, and sailing schools for all levels of experience (tel: 02 9280-1110; www.sydneybysail.com). Powerboats can be chartered, with or without a professional skipper. Try Sydney Harbour Boat Hire (tel: 02 9328-4748; www.sydneyharboures capes.com.au). Inland, you can command a boat on the relaxing Hawkesbury River (see page 80).

Windsurfing, stand-up paddling and kayaking. Botany Bay is a popular windsurfing location. Balmoral Sailing School offers windsurfing, kayaking and paddle-surfing instructions and excursions (tel: 02 9960-5344; www.sailingschool.com.au). Stand-up paddling has been described as surfing with training wheels. Standing on a very stable board, you use an elongated kayak-style

---

⊘ WALKING ABOVE SYDNEY

Two companies offer tours that require a good head for heights: **BridgeClimb** (tel: 02 8274-7777; www.bridgeclimb.com) conducts guided walks for small groups over the massive arches of the Sydney Harbour Bridge. There are three walks which vary in length of time depending on whether you climb the inner or outer arches. From Circular Quay, you can spot the climbers, looking like a row of ambitious ants, at the top of the bridge.

Far above the Bridgeclimbers are the Skywalkers of Sydney Tower (www.sydneytowereye.com.au). The viewing platform is twice as high as the Harbour Bridge. Bridgeclimbers see all of Sydney. Skywalkers get a panoramic view of the Blue Mountains and Manly. **Skywalk** (tel: 02 9333-9222; currently closed until further notice) advertises itself as 'an exhilarating outdoor walk on the roof of the city'. Participants are harnessed to walkways on the edge of the tower's turret, where they walk across a glass-floored viewing platform.

paddle to propel yourself. It takes about 10 minutes to learn the technique. Bundeena Kayak has the boards for rental and offers instruction (tel: 0419 254 981; www.bundeenakayaks.com.au). Sydney Harbour Kayaks conducts guided kayak tours of Sydney Harbour (tel: 02 9960-4389; www.sydneyharbourkayaks.com.au). **Golf.** Sydney is full of parks – closer inspection reveals that many are in fact golf courses. Among the courses that welcome visiting duffers are Moore Park Golf Course (tel: 02 9663-1064; www.mooreparkgolf.com.au) and Northbridge Golf Club (tel: 02 9958-6900; www.northbridgegolfclub.com.au). Eastlake Golf Club is one of the Top 100 courses and invites visitors (tel: 02 9663-1374; www.eastlakegolfclub.com.au).

SPECTATOR SPORTS

Rugby. Rugby League is the main event in Sydney. It is a free-flowing game with 13-player teams and crunching tackles. Rugby Union, with teams of 15, has more complex passages of play, with 8-man scrums and skilful passing. The main ground for both codes was the Sydney Football Stadium, near Centennial Park, however, this is currently closed for redevelopment and is due to reopen in 2020. Aussie Rules Football combines elements of rugby and Gaelic football. Look for long-distance kicks and passes and high scores on a large, circular field with 18 players a side.

Football. Sydney has the Sydney Football Club, Sydney City Soccer Club and Sydney United Football Club, as well as amateur

Putting on a show

In 1789, just a year after New South Wales was founded, a troupe of convict actors put on a Restoration comedy (*The Recruiting Officer*) by George Farquhar as part of the celebrations for the birthday of King George III.

Ornate interiors at The State Theatre

men's and women's leagues, plus school teams. Venues vary from school pitches to the stadium at Olympic Park.

Cricket. Cricket is an Australian passion, and the country has produced some of the world's greatest players. The traditional five-day Test matches draw thousands of fans to the Sydney Cricket Ground every summer. One-day cricket and Twenty20 take less time.

Horseracing. The races in Sydney are a glorious spectacle. Sydney has four courses: Canterbury Park, Rosehill Gardens, Warwick Farm and Royal Randwick.

ENTERTAINMENT

Free weekly guides that provide details of various alternative music and dance attractions are available at many inner-city pubs and bookshops.

Bangarra Dance Theatre

Theatre. Sydney has a flourishing theatre scene covering mainstream and alternative productions. Many of the venues are restored classic theatres. The State Theatre (tel: 02 9373-6655; www.statetheatre.com.au), with its glorious mix of Gothic, Italian, Art Deco and Australian design, and the Capitol (tel: 02 9320-5000; http://capitoltheatre.com.au), known for its staircases and Italianate interior, are almost as popular for their tours as for the performances. The Sydney Lyric Theatre in the Star City Entertainment Complex is a modern venue which attracts concerts by top performers and major shows. One of the most successful and the oldest continually running professional theatre companies in Australia is the Ensemble Theatre in Kirribilli (tel: 02 9929-0644; www.ensemble.com.au). The city's leading theatre group is the Sydney Theatre Company (tel: 02 9250-1777; www.sydneytheatre.com.au), which stages its plays mainly at the Wharf Theatre, the nearby Sydney Theatre and the

Opera House Drama Theatre. Its repertoire features many works by Australian and contemporary international playwrights. Due to redevelopment of the Wharf the theatre will perform at four different venues across Sydney in 2019 and will reopen at the Wharf in 2020. The Belvoir Theatre (tel: 02 9699-3444; www.belvoir.com.au), in Surry Hills, is known for its production of innovative, cutting-edge work. The Bell Shakespeare Company (tel: 02 8298-9000; www.bellshakespeare.com.au), based at the Opera House Drama Theatre, interprets the Bard in contemporary Australian terms. It might be worth checking out 505 Theatre in Surry Hills (www.venue505.com). This iconic music venue added an intimate space for independent theatre.

Opera. Opera Australia (tel: 02 9699-1099; www.opera-australia.org.au) performs classic, forgotten and contemporary titles at the Sydney Opera House.

Dance. Sydney Dance Company (tel: 02 9221-4811; www.sydneydancecompany.com) is the city's foremost modern dance troupe. Its new venue is the Sydney Theatre at The Wharf in Walsh Bay however, due to redevelopment performances will be held at the Ultimo studio during 2019. The Bangarra Dance Theatre (tel: 02 9251-5333; www.bangarra.com.au) draws upon the culture and traditions of Australia's Aboriginal people for inspiration. Performances are usually at the Opera House and sell out quickly. The Australian Ballet (tel: 1300 369-741; www.australianballet.com.au) is known for its versatility, technical excellence and unpretentious style. Based in Melbourne, the Opera House is its home when in Sydney.

Concerts. The three primary venues for classic and concert music are Sydney Opera House (www.sydneyoperahouse.com), the City Recital Hall (known for its excellent acoustics; tel: 02 8256-2222; www.cityrecitalhall.com) and the Sydney Conservatorium of Music (tel: 02 9351-1222). They welcome

Sydney's rich musical talents like the Philharmonia Choirs (tel: 02 8274-6200) and Sydney Symphony Orchestra (tel: 02 8215-4600; www.sydneysymphony.com), as well as visiting performers from elsewhere in Australia and the world.

Other live music. Jazz, blues and rock bands play at pubs and clubs all over the city. The Vanguard in Newtown is world-renowned for its jazz, blues, cabaret and Aussie-inspired artists (tel: 02 9557-7992; www.thevanguard.com.au). Venue 505 in Surry Hills showcases world music, Latin, jazz and mellow fusion (www.venue505.com).

Cinema. In central Sydney, George Street has multi-screen cinema complexes that show popcorn movies. Less mainstream films are shown at the Dendy Opera Quays, at a great location near the Opera House, and in Paddington at the Academy Twin, the Verona and the Chauvel. Two outdoor cinemas put Sydney's summer evenings to good use: the Moonlight Cinema (www.moonlight.com.au), in Centennial Park's Amphitheatre, and the OpenAir Cinema (www.stgeorgeopenair.com.au) in the Royal Botanic Gardens facing the Opera House.

MARDI GRAS

Sydney is one of the world's most hospitable cities for gay visitors. The best-known gay and lesbian event in Australia is the Sydney **Gay and Lesbian Mardi Gras Parade**, which takes place each February. The climactic finale of a month-long festival of gay art, culture, music, theatre and dance, the parade culminates in a wild party. Tickets to the party usually sell out before the end of January, but you don't need a ticket to watch the parade.

SYDNEY FESTIVAL

The **Sydney Festival** (www.sydneyfestival.org.au) in January is one of the premier cultural events in the world. It's a three-week celebration of music, dance, visual and performing arts, attracting an audience of over 1 million people. Over 300 free and ticketed performances are staged at 20 different venues during the festival. The festival attracts international opera stars, avant-garde theatre companies, independent cinema, circuses and dancers; even Sydney Harbour ferries join forces with local acts to entertain crowds.

New Year's Eve fireworks

The **Sydney Fringe Festival**, held in September, is an irreverent three-week alternative cultural festival centered in casual, multicultural Newtown.

NIGHTLIFE

Sydney's nightlife is dazzling in its scope and variety. If you're looking for a relaxed evening out in a period setting, **The Rocks** is the place to be. Try the historic Lord Nelson Brewery Hotel, 19 Kent Street, or The Hero of Waterloo, 81 Lower Fort. The Shangri-La Hotel's classy top-floor Blu Horizon Bar, 176 Cumberland Street, has sensational views of the harbour. A little further afield, **Bondi Beach** offers a seaside atmosphere and great views of the Pacific. Bar 34 Bondi has a comfortable atmosphere, and it's a chance to hang with the locals while you enjoy live music and refreshments.

On **Oxford Street**, Slide is one of the most unusual nightclubs in Sydney. There are three shows: a Parisian-style cabaret dinner theatre in the style of Cirque du Soleil; an intimate caba-ret; and 'Vampire Stories', a Vegas-style revue with elements of *Rocky Horror* (not for children). Reviewers give both the food and the performances high marks (tel: 02 8915-1899; www.slide.com.au). Dance clubs with DJs and live bands line the streets in Cockle Bay Wharf, Darling Harbour and King Street Wharf.

Casino. The Star City casino complex is located in Pyrmont, just around the corner from Darling Harbour. It has a full range of table games, Keno, an elegant Baccarat Room, and off-track betting with large monitors where bettors can watch the races.

The Entertainment Quarter on Lang Road near Centennial Park (www.eqmoorepark.com.au) contains cinemas and plenty of cafés, restaurants and bars.

CHILDREN'S SYDNEY

Sydney has many activities to engage the kids. Several child-friendly attractions are conveniently located in **Darling Harbour** (see page 50): Sydney Aquarium, Sydney Wildlife World, Tumbalong Park and, for older children, the Imax Theatre, the Powerhouse Museum and the Maritime Museum. **Taronga Zoo** (see page 30) and **Featherdale Wildlife Park** (see page 66) appeal to kids of all ages. The 'Search and Discover' section on the second floor of the **Australian Museum** (see page 49) lets children get their hands on all sorts of exciting exhibits. **Luna Park** is a vintage amusement park from the 1930s at Milsons Point. The **Opera House** (see page 39) runs events such as the Babies Proms, which allows toddlers to get close to the musical instruments (tel: 02 9250-7777). The **Art Gallery of New South Wales** (see page 42) holds family events on Sundays, such as renditions of Aboriginal Dreamtime stories (tel: 1800-679-278).

CALENDAR OF EVENTS

January. Sydney Festival: a month of Australian and international music, dance, theatre and the visual arts. Big Day Out: alternative music festival at Sydney Showground. Manly Surf Carnival: surf carnival attracting thousands of entrants at Manly Beach. Australia Day (26 January): celebration of Australia's national day, with events at Darling Harbour and a ferry race on Sydney Harbour.

March–April. Sydney Gay and Lesbian Mardi Gras Parade: fun-filled, provocative parade along Oxford Street. Sydney Cup: major Sydney horse race, held at Randwick Racecourse. Royal Easter Show: agricultural displays and carnival rides at Sydney Olympic Park. Anzac Day parade (25 April): old soldiers march down George Street to remember Australians killed in war. Canberra Balloon Fiesta: more than 60 hot-air balloons take to the skies over the nation's capital in April.

May. Sydney Writers' Festival: major literary festival attracting Australian and international authors.

June. Sydney Biennale: contemporary visual arts festival held in even-numbered years. Sydney Film Festival: major Australian film festival. Sydney Good Food and Wine Fair: held at Darling Harbour.

August. City to Surf fun run: thousands of contestants run from the city to Bondi Beach, a distance of about 14km (8.75 miles).

September. Sydney Fringe Festival. Festival of the Winds: kite-flying festival held at Bondi Beach.

October. Manly International Jazz Festival. Good Food Month: celebrating the food and wine industries of New South Wales at various central city locations. Floriade (Canberra): month-long festival of spring flowers, starts end September.

November. Sculpture by the Sea: outdoor sculpture exhibition along the walking track from Bondi to Bronte.

December. Homebake: Sydney's major rock festival, held in The Domain. Sydney to Hobart yacht race: one of the world's toughest yacht races, starting on Boxing Day. New Year's Eve: superb fireworks displays on the harbour; party in The Rocks.

EATING OUT

Modern Australian cuisine – sometimes called 'Mod Oz' – takes fresh, high-quality ingredients and combines them with culinary approaches and techniques borrowed from all over the world. Sydney's dynamic food culture is a pleasant by-product of two influences: the various ethnic groups that make up the population and a climate that allows a wide range of food to be cultivated locally.

WHAT TO EAT AND DRINK

Immigrants from countries as diverse as Italy and Malaysia have revolutionised the urban Sydney diet, transforming it from basic meat-and-veg fodder to fusion food, a collage of culinary influences from Asia, the Mediterranean and the Middle East. Australian chefs have created perhaps the most sophisticated and innovative cuisine in the world – quite a feat in a land where Vegemite is an ubiquitous, treasured kitchen condiment.

Chefs in Sydney have the advantage of being able to work with superb raw materials. Australia's size and climatic diversity make it possible to produce an astonishing variety of fruits and vegetables – apples, lychees, mandarins, custard apples,

⊘ WILL WALK FOR FOOD

Food-lovers can taste all of Sydney's culinary experiences on a food tour. Ultimately Sydney offers a three hour walking tour presenting some of the locals favourite hangouts as well as informing on historical information about the city (tel: 02-9238 6888; www.ultimatelysydney.com.au).

mangoes, strawberries, blackberries, passionfruit, pumpkin (squash) and bok choy – to name just a few. Top-quality meat and a wide range of super-fresh seafood add to the classy culinary mix. Chefs never have to venture too far to find ingredients which combine to produce astounding results that would be hard to duplicate anywhere else in the world.

Harbourside dining

Dining in Sydney can be as expensive as you want it to be. Good food does not necessarily mean expensive. Foodies agree that the city's top-level restaurants compare in quality to the best restaurants in New York, Paris and London – with prices to match. Pretty much any establishment that offers a view of the harbour will be considerably more expensive than a restaurant of similar quality lacking a view. But moderately priced restaurants abound in Sydney, even in areas most popular with tourists and in the inner suburbs. Fast-food franchises are not particularly popular and are not easy to find. Note that smoking is banned in all restaurants.

Bush tucker

Australian chefs often try to incorporate native food into their dishes. Ingredients such as muntari berries, bush tomatoes, Illawarra plums, lemon myrtle and lilli pillies have begun

First vines

Australia may have been intended as a brutal penal colony, but that did not mean the authorities in charge intended to suffer. The First Fleet stopped at the Cape of Good Hope on its voyage so that Governor Phillip could collect vine cuttings to start vineyards in Australia. By 1820 wine was available for sale domestically.

to appear on restaurant menus, often blended with traditional dishes of meat and fish. This native food of Australia – the fruits, seeds, nuts, fungi, mammals, reptiles, fish and birds that sustained Aborigines for tens of thousands of years – is referred to collectively as 'bush tucker'. Popular ingredients include quandongs (similar to a peach but with a rhubarb-like tang), wattle seeds (sometimes used in ice cream to give a coffee-like flavour), Kakadu plums (less sweet than the usual variety) and bunya bunya nuts (delicious in satay sauces). Kangaroo, crocodile and emu (a relative of the ostrich) have also found their way onto many menus; all three are commercially farmed and are low in fat. Two Aboriginal foods that have yet to become popular in Sydney restaurants – and let's face it, probably never will – are witchetty grubs (large grubs found in the trunks and roots of wattle trees) and bogong moths (a hefty migratory moth, usually roasted in a fire and eaten like peanuts).

Australian wines

Australian wines are among the world's best – a judgement confirmed regularly at international wine shows. Wine is produced in every state in Australia over a great range of climatic and soil conditions. Australia is best known for Shiraz (known in Europe as Syrah), Cabernet Sauvignon and Merlot. Chardonnay, Semillon and Riesling are the most popular whites. Winemakers are beginning to plant grapes new to Australia, although familiar elsewhere. Pinot Noir and Chenin Blanc are examples of this evolution.

Many of Sydney's less expensive restaurants are BYO (bring your own). Bottle shops (off licences) are not hard to find, and most offer a wide selection at very moderate prices. Most BYO restaurants charge a corkage fee, and staff are obligated to serve the alcohol.

The amber nectar

Beer (aka the amber nectar) is served cold, sometimes very cold. The alcoholic strength of Australian beer must by law be displayed on the can or bottle. Full-strength draught beer is around 4.9 percent alcohol, 'mid-strength' beer will be around 3.5 percent alcohol and beers marked 'light' will be no more than 2.7 percent alcohol.

Hunter Valley red wine crops

Major commercial brands popular in Sydney include Tooheys, Squires, Hahn and Victoria Bitter. But 'boutique' beers are becoming increasingly popular. About a dozen small breweries are located in and around Sydney. Lord Nelson Brewery Hotel, Redoak

Alfresco dining at the Opera Bar

Brewery, Schwartz Brewery – all in Sydney – and 4 Pines in Manly, brew on-site. They carry other microbrews from all over Australia, as does The Harts Pub and the Australian Hotel.

A 285ml (10-ounce) beer glass is called a 'middie' in New South Wales and a 425ml (15-ounce) glass is called a 'schooner'. A small bottle of beer is known throughout Australia as a 'stubbie'. An off licence is called a bottle shop, or 'bottle-o'.

WHERE TO EAT

Some of Sydney's most acclaimed restaurants are to be found in The Rocks, around Circular Quay, in the CBD and along Victoria Street. The area's pubs serve traditional pub food as well as creative meals that reflect Sydney's diverse population. Australians love pizza; you'll find almost anything served on a thin crust. The Australian Hotel is the place to go to try kangaroo, crocodile or emu pizza. Darling Harbour and the adjoining Cockle Bay and King Street wharves also boast a smorgasbord of restaurant options which are popular with tourists. Don't limit your dining to these areas, though, because many other neighbourhoods and suburbs such as Kings Cross, Balmain, Surry Hills, Darlinghurst, Paddington and Newtown offer exciting options as well. The restaurants in the inner suburbs and residential neighbourhoods cater to the local residents. Many of the small ethnic restaurants are family affairs, offering outstanding cuisine at moderate prices.

It is nearly impossible to define one neighbourhood by its cuisine, with the exception of Leichhardt. This is the heart of Sydney's Italian community, and the pleasant aroma of simmering Marinara sauce and garlic bread wafts along Marion and Norton Streets. Newtown may have the most eclectic selection of ethnic restaurants. A stroll down King Street takes you past Thai, Greek, Nepalese, Japanese, Modern Oz, Indian, Vegetarian, basic burgers and general pub grub. The proximity of the University of Sydney, with its population of impecunious students, means that prices are typically moderate, if not downright cheap.

Bondi Beach and Manly are known for their waterfront dining options, particularly their seafood and Mod Oz selections.

⊘ FIRST BREWER

James Squire, a convict transported to Australia on the First Fleet for stealing, is credited with the first successful cultivation of hops in Australia and for opening the first brewery. So appreciated were his accomplishments that they were noted on his headstone. The James Squire beers are named in his honour.

Top dining

Sydney boasts one of the best restaurants in the world, with Quay consistently claiming a spot on The World's 50 Best Restaurants extended list for nine editions. Book well in advance – you may want to book the restaurant before you book your airline flight if a visit is on the agenda.

On the North Shore, Crows Nest, McMahon's Point and Kirribilli are the best bets.

Sydney Fish Market

Sydney's bustling Fish Market, on Blackwattle Bay in Pyrmont (just west of Darling Harbour), is well worth a visit. Australian tuna, Tasmanian salmon and blue swimmer crabs are all air-freighted from here to Japan, where they appear on the auction block at Tokyo's Tsukiji Market not long after they are hauled from the sea. But much of the daily catch stays right there in Sydney, to be sold at the market's daily early-morning auction (wholesale only) or throughout the day at the many retail outlets that line the wharf.

You can easily put together a fine seafood meal by grazing your way past the sushi bars, fish cafés and vendors offering everything from fresh, ice-cold raw oysters to grilled mixed-seafood platters (prepared alfresco). One of the best-value lunches is the simplest. Just ask for a kilo (2.2lbs) of large cooked prawns (shrimps) and pick a bottle of crisp white wine from a bottle shop. Grab a seat at one of the tables on the dock and savour your meal while boats bob at anchor and pelicans soar overhead.

There are few places in the world where you'll be able to see as many types of freshwater fish, saltwater fish and shellfish amassed in one place. The displays are overwhelming and many visitors find it hard to choose.

Be adventurous and try something new, like 'bugs', for example. Balmain bugs are a type of saltwater crustacean, similar to crayfish; they're highly favoured by Sydneysiders. Other popular choices are yabbies (native freshwater crayfish), Tasmanian lobsters, baby octopus, freshwater barramundi and king prawns (shrimp). You might even come across crocodile fillets from Darwin.

You can experience the dynamic activity of the market first hand on the daily tour. While you'll have to prepare yourself for an early start – the tour begins at 6.40am. It really is a fantastic experience, and you'll be taken down onto the auction floor, in the middle of the orchestrated chaos of the daily sale (tel: 02 9004-1108; www.sydneyfishmarket.com.au; Mon–Fri; reservations required).

A fresh catch at Sydney Fish Market

PLACES TO EAT

We have used the following symbols to give an idea of the price for a three-course meal for one, excluding drinks and tip:

$$$$	over AU$100
$$$	AU$75–100
$$	AU$40–75
$	below AU$40

THE ROCKS AND CIRCULAR QUAY

Altitude $$$$ *Atop the Shangri-La Hotel, 176 Cumberland Street, tel: 02 9250-6123, www.36levelsabove.com.au.* There is no better view of the city than from the floor-to-ceiling windows at this award-winning restaurant on the 36th floor. If the average AU$100+ per person for a meal is a bit steep, enjoy the view from Blu Bar. Average cocktail is AU$20. Beers are around AU$10.

Bistro Guillaume $$$$ *259 George Street, CBD, tel: 02 8622-9555,* www.bistroguillaumesydney.com.au. This is one of the city's best restaurants. The setting is elegant and sophisticated and so is the food. The focus is on seasonal, produce-driven food.

The Bridge Room $$$ *44 Bridge Street, The Rocks, tel: 02 9247-7000,* www,thebridgeroom.com.au. Housed in a 1930s building but decorated in contemporary style, this elegant restaurant offers a unique perspective on dining. Choose between the a la carte or tasting menu both if which present modern Australian dishes.

Fish at The Rocks $$$$ *29 Kent Street, The Rocks, tel: 02 9252-4614,* www.fishattherocks.com.au. Traditional dishes are presented in an artful way at one of Sydney's favourite seafood restaurants, which was established in 1988. An early bird menu is available.

Lord Nelson Brewery Hotel $$ *19 Kent Street, The Rocks, tel: 02 9251-4044,* www.lordnelsonbrewery.com. The first-floor brasserie serves an innovative menu – sage and beef rigatoni, confit of rabbit legs with star anise – alongside an in-depth wine list.

Quay $$$$ *upper level, Overseas Passenger Terminal, George Street & Argyle Street, The Rocks, tel: 02-9251-5600,* www.quay.com.au. The breathtaking harbour setting is matched with a very good, modern Australian menu. The chef, Peter Gilmore, looks to nature for his inspiration and makes imaginative use of local ingredients.

Shiki $$$$ *Corner of Argyle and Harrington Street, tel: 02 9252-2431,* www.shiki.com.au. One of the most interesting Japanese restaurants in Sydney serving Teppanyaki cuisine and colourful unique cocktails. Menus change seasonally.

CITY CENTRE

Beppi's $$ *21 Yurong Street, tel: 02 9360-4558,* www.beppis.com.au. Traditional Italian food in the heart of Sydney. Beppi's serves fresh seafood, home-made pasta and meat dishes with gluten-free options also available. Their zucchini flowers, spinach ravioli or gnocchi with prawns are all worth a try.

Billy Kwong $$ *Shop 1, 28 Macleay Street, Potts Point, tel: 02 9332-3300,* www.kyliekwong.org. Chef Kylie Kwong celebrates the flavours and textures of traditional Chinese cuisine in this intimate (tiny) restaurant. Reservations necessary.

Bistro Papillon $$ *98 Clarence Street, tel: 02 9262-2402,* www.bistropapillon.com.au. A classy, welcoming bistro with true French country cuisine. The set menus for lunch and dinner are good value.

Encasa $$ *423 Pitt Street, tel: 02 9211-4257,* www.encasa.com.au. A well-liked Spanish restaurant with great specials. The paella is tasty and authentic (but takes 45 minutes to prepare).

Est. $$$$ *252 George Street in the Establishment Hotel, tel: 02 9240-3000,* www.merivale.com. Chef Peter Doyle is considered the Father of Mod-

ern Australian cuisine. His innovative treatment of native ingredients is served with panache in a surprisingly sterile dining room. The tasting menu is slightly more affordable.

Hyde Park Barracks Café $$ *Queens Square, Macquarie Street, tel: 02 9222-1815*, www.hydeparkbarrackscafe.com.au. Located in former convict barracks. Breakfast here includes tea, hot meals or smoothies – more substantial dishes are served at lunch.

Medusa Greek Taverna $$ *2 Market Street (corner of Market and Kent streets), tel: 02 9267-0799*, www.medusagreektaverna.com.au. A great place for lovers of authentic, creative Greek cuisine. The contemporary setting accommodates groups of four or more with a Greek banquet, served family-style.

Mode Kitchen and Bar $$$ *199 George Street in the Four Seasons Hotel, tel: 02 9250-3160*, www.fourseasons.com/sydney. Contemporary Australian cuisine with a strong Mediterranean influence served in a beautiful 1920s-inspired setting. The perfect balance between casual bistro and fine dining.

DARLING HARBOUR/COCKLE BAY/CHINATOWN

BBQ King $$ *76-78 Liverpool Street, tel: 02 9267-2433*. BBQ King is nearly legendary for its duck and pork dishes Try the hot and sour soup, a delicate mélange of flavours.

Hurricane's Grill & Bar $$ *Level 2, Harbourside Shopping Centre, Darling Harbour, tel: 02 9211-2210*, www.hurricanesgrill.com.au. Back to basics: steaks, ribs, BBQ chicken, beef, pork, and lamb and fresh salads. Chicken wings and garlic mushrooms.

Lindt Chocolat Café $ *103 Cockle Bay Wharf, tel: 02 9267- 8064*. Chocolate pastries, cakes, ice creams and confections, and a view of the water; this café is definitely one to try.

Sailmaker $$$ *161 Sussex Street, Hyatt Hotel, tel: 02 8099-1234*, www. hyatt.com. Sailmaker offers a truly local experience: fresh prawns and fish from the Sydney fish market and grilled meat from NSW are used to crete the modern Australian menu.

EASTERN SUBURBS

Aki's $$ *6 Cowper Wharf Road, Woolloomooloo, tel: 02 9332-4600*, www.akisindian.com.au. This is one of the best Indian restaurants in the city. The menu features dishes from various parts of India. Set meals for four or more people cost AU$68–78 per person, depending on the menu. Get a table outside for harbour views.

Bill's $$ *433 Liverpool Street, Darlinghurst, tel: 02 9360-9631*, www.bills.com.au. This renowned café-restaurant serves great-value breakfasts, lunches and dinners. Its signature dishes include ricotta hotcakes with honeycomb butter. It's very busy at weekends.

Chinta Kechil $$ *342 New South Head Road, Double Bay; tel: 02 9327-8888*, www.chintakechil.com. Enjoy Malaysian food from an extensive menu, both old favourites (nasi goreng, gado gado) and new dishes.

Erciyes $$ *409 Cleveland Street, Surry Hills, tel: 02 9319-1309*, www.erciyesrestaurant.com.au. Cheap, cheerful and well-patronised Turkish restaurant specialising in *pide* (Turkish pizza). Reservations are recommended at weekends, when belly dancers perform. There's a AU$50-55 per person banquet deal at weekends.

Harry's Café de Wheels $ *Corner of Cowper Wharf Road and Brougham Road, Woolloomooloo, tel: 02 9357-3074*, www.harryscafedewheels.com.au. This restaurant has been serving meat pies in all varieties since 1938. The authentic Aussie tucker serves workers, regulars and the odd celebrity before noon until the early hours.

Longrain $$ *85 Commonwealth Street, Surry Hills, tel: 02 9280- 2888*, www.longrain.com.au. A fashionable crowd flocks to this restaurant for the superb modern Thai cuisine. Dishes include snapper in a red curry sauce and caramelised pork hock served at communal tables.

Original Balkan Restaurant $$ *249 Crown Street, Darlinghurst, tel: 02 9331-7670*, www.balkanrestaurant.com.au. Croatian owners combined their traditional recipes with the fresh seafood and locally grown produce to create some tasty dishes.

INNER WEST

Badde Manors Café $ *37 Glebe Point Road, Glebe, tel: 02 9660-3797*, www.baddemanorscafe.com. Enjoy good, international vegetarian food throughout the day at this long-established café.

Gigi Pizzeria $ *379 King Street, Newtown, tel: 02-9557-2224*, www.gigipizzeria.com.au. Praised widely as having 'the best pizza outside Italy', Gigi takes the food seriously. Received a prestigious award from the True Neapolitan Pizza Association.

Hartsyard $$$ *33 Enmore Road, Newton, tel: 02 8068-1473*, www.hartsyard.com.au. The restaurant serves a large selection of snacks and larger dishes designed for sharing. Three chef's menus are available ($78 or $95 per person, $68 for the vegetarian option).

La Botte D'oro $$ *137 Marion Stret, Leichhardt, tel: 02 9560-1349*, www.labottedoro.com. A great trattoria with the lively feel of a family dining room. Classic dishes and Australian seafood are all given the Italian treatment (the pizzas are particularly good).

Oscillate Wildly $$$$ *275 Australia Street, Newtown, tel: 02 9517-4700*, www.oscillatewildly.com.au. The former chef at Est. has won over restaurant and food critics, with the awards to prove it. A nine-course seasonal meal is offered ($250 per person). Option to add wine pairings for additional cost.

THE BEACHES
Bondi

Barzura $$ *62 Carr Street, Coogee, tel: 02 9665-5546*, www.barzura.com.au. Watch the sun rise over the Pacific and return for lunch, dinner or a late-night drink. Modern Australian cooking, with influences ranging from Greek to Cajun. The appealing view across Coogee Beach adds extra sparkle.

Pompei's $$ *126–130 Roscoe Street, Bondi Beach, tel: 02 9365-1233*, www. pompeis.com.au. A very popular restaurant featuring authentic Italian pasta and over 25 varieties of pizza. The delicious fruit sorbets and tasty gelatos make this outlet worth a visit alone; they are made fresh daily with fruit that is in season.

Sean's Panaroma $$$ *270 Campbell Parade, Bondi Beach, tel: 02 9365-4924.* A totally unique eatery with a menu that changes daily to reflect what's fresh in from the local farms and docks. At least four choices for each course are offered, or try the chef's menu for AU$110 (AU$145 with wine).

Manly

Maestro and Co $$$$ *50 East Esplanade, Manly, tel: 02 9976-3065*, www. maestroandco.com.au. Great tapas with a Lebanese twist is on offer here with larger plates are also available including beef borek, vege tagine and many others.

Watsons Bay

Doyle's on the Beach $$$$ *11 Marine Parade, tel: 02 9337-2007*, www. doyles.com.au. A chance to enjoy a million-dollar view is offered at the popular spot, and there are prices to match. The emphasis is on seafood, which is prepared simply and presented beautifully to the beachside tables.

A–Z TRAVEL TIPS

A SUMMARY OF PRACTICAL INFORMATION

A

ACCOMMODATION (see also Camping and Youth hostels)

Accommodation in Sydney ranges from hostels and rooms above pubs to large international hotels. Depending on the location and amenities, lodging can range from surprisingly affordable to dazzlingly expensive. Large five-star hotels can easily cost AU$500/night. Moderately priced, conveniently situated hotels in The Rocks or CBD average around AU$180/night. There is excellent accommodation a short bus ride away in the suburbs, which is even less expensive.

Tourism Australia (www.australia.com) has a hotel finder that breaks down listings by ratings, location and price range with links to websites. You can reserve accommodation through your travel agent, airline or online. Within Australia, book through the state tourist offices, domestic airlines, hotel chains or through online providers such as Wotif (www.wotif.com) or Sydney Online Reservations (www.sydneyreservations.com). Accommodation may be harder to find during the Australian school holidays. These are staggered state by state except for at the year-end (Dec–Feb), when schools everywhere close. Tourism Australia offices can provide details (see page 115).

AIRPORTS

Sydney Airport (SYD; www.sydneyairport.com.au), about 8km (5 miles) from the city centre, is Australia's busiest international airport. The domestic and international terminals are a shuttle-bus ride apart. There is a railway line between the airport and Sydney's Central Station. This Airport Link (www.airportlink.com.au) has ten stations, including one at Sydney Airport's international terminal and another at the domestic terminal. There is also a freeway linking central Sydney with the airport.

Arriving passengers can travel from Sydney Airport to town by taxi (30 minutes), train (15 minutes) or bus (30–40 minutes). The Airporter bus service (tel: 02 8339-0155; www.kst.com.au) goes to major hotels.

A shuttle service is also available through Sydney Maxi Cabs (www.city shuttle.com.au) or Easy Shuttle (www.easyshuttle.com.au).

B

BICYCLE RENTAL

Attempts to cater to Sydney's sizeable cycling fraternity have often resulted in little more than cosmetic changes. Bicycle lanes are marked on some inner-city roads, but most drivers ignore them. Many drain covers have slots that run parallel to the kerb, so cycle carefully. Cyclists must by law wear helmets. Several bike tours are on offer (Bonza Bike Tours offers escorted trips around Sydney and Manly Beach; tel: 02 9247-8800). For bike rentals, try Centennial Park Cycles (tel: 02 9398-5027).

BUDGETING FOR YOUR TRIP

Sydney is one of the more expensive cities on the planet, but with some budgeting and planning, you can easily enjoy the city without scrimping. A meal at a moderately priced restaurant is AU$20. A bottle of Australian wine from a bottle shop (off licence) starts at about $10, a 425ml glass of beer in a pub costs from AU$6 and a cup of coffee or tea costs about AU$4. Entry to a museum or art gallery ranges from free up to AU$25 per person. Combination tickets to attractions can help reduce costs, and many hotels offer discount packages.

Transport costs. Air travel to Australia is still relatively expensive, but domestic airfares are getting more reasonable, thanks to competition. International passengers may be entitled to discounted travel within Australia, depending on their airline and type of fare. On the ground, train travel can be competitive over shorter distances. Trainlink (www.transportnsw.info), the NSW State Rail and coach service, offers an adult economy return trip to Canberra for about AU$50. Coach travel is generally cheaper – try Greyhound Australia (www.greyhound.com.au).

The rough cost of a half-day coach sightseeing tour is AU$55–80 per person. A tour of the Blue Mountains costs AU$90–150.

The average cost of a litre of petrol (gasoline) is approximately AU$1.50. Hiring a medium-sized car costs from AU$90 per day, and hiring a camper van (sleeping two) costs about AU$600 per week. Caravan park sites often charge less than AU$25 a night.

C

CAMPING

Australians are avid campers, and you'll find campsites all over the country. The sites tend to be packed during school holidays. They all have at least the basic amenities, and in some cases much more in the way of comfort. Aside from roomy tents with lights and floors, some installations have caravans (trailers) or cabins. Showers, toilets, laundry facilities and barbecue grills are commonly available. Sheets and blankets can often be hired. The national parks generally have well-organised camping facilities. To camp beyond the designated zone you must ask rangers for permission. The Basin scenic campsite on the shore of Pittwater in Ku-ring-gai Chase National Park, quite close to the city, is a favourite. Many coach tours include camping, or you can hire a camper van or motor home by the day or week.

CAR HIRE

In inner-city Sydney, with its traffic jams and parking hassles, a car is a burden. To travel at your own pace, however, there's no substitute for a car or a four-wheel-drive vehicle. Competition among car rental companies means you can often find deals. Unlimited mileage is common, and there are often weekend discounts. Expect to pay from AU$350 per week for a medium-sized car and from AU$600/week for a two-berth camper van.

If you intend to drive in remote country areas, rates may be considerably higher. It's worth shopping around, but be careful – some companies impose a metropolitan limit on vehicles. Check first, as your insurance won't be valid outside the designated area.

To hire a car you'll need a current driving licence. The minimum age is 21, or in some cases 25. Third-party insurance is included; collision damage and personal accident insurance will cost extra. US travellers should confirm that their coverage for this is valid in Australia.

Big firms such as Avis, Hertz, Thrifty and Budget offer interstate arrangements where you pick up a car in one city and return it elsewhere. Camper vans and caravans are also available, although you may find they are reserved far in advance for school holiday periods.

CLIMATE

Sydney enjoys a temperate and pleasant climate. It's not perfect; late-summer humidity, which runs at an average 69 percent, makes Sydney the most humid Australian city outside tropical Darwin. Ocean breezes help cool Sydney's coastal suburbs. Seasons are the reverse of those in the northern hemisphere, with winter running from June to August. Rain tends to fall in intense, tropical bursts in summer. February and March are sultry months, ideal for mosquitoes. April and May are more pleasant. The NSW Outback is very hot from December to February.

Average Sydney temperatures are as follows:

		J	F	M	A	M	J	J	A	S	O	N	D
Max	°C	26	26	25	22	19	17	16	18	20	22	24	25
Min	°C	18	19	17	15	11	9	8	9	11	13	15	17
Max	°F	79	79	77	72	66	63	61	64	68	72	75	77
Min	°F	64	66	63	59	52	48	46	48	52	55	59	63
Ocean temperature													
	°C	22	22	22	21	14	17	16	16	16	17	19	20
	°F	72	72	72	70	58	63	61	61	61	63	66	68

CLOTHING

A light raincoat will serve in almost any season. A sweater or fleece will come in handy in winter, and you'll need comfortable walking shoes. While Sydneysiders dress casually at weekends, business attire can be surprisingly conservative. Restaurants do not require men to wear a jacket and tie, but some may refuse customers wearing T-shirts, vest tops, ripped jeans or thongs (flip-flops). Nightclubs generally require a collared shirt and smart shoes – not trainers or flip-flops.

CRIME AND SAFETY

Sydney's murder rate is low by world standards and the city is generally safe. It's still wise to take the usual precautions against burglary and petty theft, and be on the alert for pickpockets in crowded areas. It's also wise to avoid Hyde Park after dark, particularly if on your own. William Street, which runs from Hyde Park to Kings Cross, is another place where it's unwise to loiter after dark. The secluded back-streets of Kings Cross have a similar reputation, although the main strip is safe enough. There have been reports of bag-snatching and fights around the Redfern Station and Waterloo areas. Kings Cross is Sydney's 'adult' entertainment area and should be visited with caution.

D

DISABLED TRAVELLERS

Most attractions, major shopping areas and restaurants are accessible to travellers with physical disabilities. Many attractions and museums provide wheelchairs at no charge, although some places ask that the user be accompanied by an assistant. Websites usually provide details of accessible entrances. The ferries have a particularly good service.

DRIVING

Australians drive on the left and pass on the right. Australian roads are good considering the size of the country and the challenges of distance, terrain and climate. Freeways and motorways link populous regions, but most country roads are a single lane which can get crowded. Within Sydney, freeways (marked with an 'F') are toll-free; motorways ('M') have a toll.

Regulations. Drivers and passengers must wear seat belts (the exception is on some buses and coaches). Car-hire companies can supply suitable child restraints, boosters and seats, at an extra charge. Tourists may drive in Australia on a valid overseas licence for the same class of vehicle. Licences must be carried when driving. If the licence is in a language other than English, the visitor must carry a translation. An International Drivers Permit is not sufficient by itself.

Speed limits are signposted. In cities, the speed limit is generally 60km/h (about 35mph), but on suburban streets it is usually 50km/h (about 30mph). In the NSW countryside, the limit is 100 or 110km/h (about 70mph). Police make random checks for drugs or alcohol, using breath tests. The limit on alcohol in the blood is 0.05, meaning in practice that two or three glasses of wine or two or three medium-size ('middy') glasses of beer in an hour will take you to the limit. If you are under 25 and in your first three years of driving, you must be under 0.02, which doesn't allow you to drink at all.

City driving. Heavy traffic and parking problems afflict the central city area and parking meters, and 'no standing' zones proliferate.

Outback driving. Driving in Australia's wilderness requires planning and awareness, as mistakes can easily lead to disaster. Many of the roads are dirt tracks, full of potholes and corrugations which can easily cause even a careful driver to lose control. Thoroughly check the condition of your car, and be sure you have a spare wheel and plenty of spare drinking water. Find out about the fuel situation in advance, and always leave word as to your destination and anticipated arrival time. If at all possible, travel with another vehicle. Your cell phone will generally be useless; rent a two-way HF radio instead. Fill up the fuel tank at every opportunity, as the next station may be a few hundred kilometres away. Obtain local knowledge about the road conditions. Be cautious with road trains, consisting of three or four huge trailers barrelling down the motorway towed by a high-powered truck. Pass one with the greatest of care. It is best to avoid driving at night, as roads are often hard to see and wildlife can be drawn to the headlights.

Fuel. Many filling stations are open only during normal shopping hours, so you may have to ask where out-of-hours service is available. Petrol (gasoline) in Australia comes in unleaded regular and premium unleaded grades, and is sold by the litre. In 2019, a litre of petrol cost about AU$1.50. Prices are often higher in country areas. Most stations are self-service and accept international credit cards.

Road signs. Signs are generally good, especially along popular roads. All distances are measured in kilometres. White-on-brown direction signs signal tourist attractions and natural wonders. Exit routes from cities are often signposted with the assumption that drivers have local experience, so you may need a good map and some advance planning. Most road signs are the standard international pictographs, but some are unique to Australia, such as silhouette images of kangaroos or wombats, warning that you may encounter these animals crossing the road. Some other signs unique to Australia include:

> **Crest** Hilltop limiting visibility
> **Cyclist hazard** Dangerous for cyclists
> **Dip** Severe depression in road surface
> **Hump** Bump or speed obstacle
> **Safety Ramp** Uphill escape lane from a steep downhill road
> **Soft Edges** Soft shoulders

E

ELECTRICITY

The standard throughout Australia is 230–250 volt, 50-cycle AC. Plugs are three-pronged, in the shape of a bird's footprint, like those used in

New Zealand. If you're from elsewhere, you'll need an adaptor. Many hotel rooms also have 110-volt outlets for razors and small appliances. You can purchase adaptors at many shops in tourist areas.

EMBASSIES AND CONSULATES

The embassies or high commissions of about 70 countries are established in Canberra. They have consular sections dealing with the general formalities. More than 40 countries also have diplomatic representation in Sydney. The following consulates are in Sydney:

Canada: Level 5, Quay West Building, 111 Harrington Street; tel: 02 9364-3000.

Ireland: Level 26, 1 Market Street; tel: 02 9264-9635.

New Zealand: Level 6, 55 Hunter Street; tel: 02 8256-2000.

UK: Level 16, The Gateway, 1 Macquarie Place; tel: 02 9247-7521.

US: Level 10, MLC Centre, 19–29 Martin Place; tel: 1300-139-399.

EMERGENCIES

For an ambulance, the fire department or the police, dial **000**. This number is free to dial from public telephones. You can also dial 112, 911 or 000 if using a mobile phone.

G

GETTING THERE

By air. Flights from Asia, North America and Europe serve international airports around Australia, of which Sydney's is the busiest. Australia is included in several 'round-the-world' fare schemes – arrangements between two or more airlines that allow passengers to travel globally at bargain rates, provided they keep to a certain mileage and number of stopovers. Flight times (approximate) are New York–Sydney, 22 hours; Los Angeles–Sydney, 15 hours; London–Sydney, 21 hours. You can usually break the flight along the way.

By sea. Sydney features in the itineraries of many cruise ships. You can fly to, say, Bali or Singapore and embark on the liner there, sail to Australia, then fly home, or resume the cruise at another port.

GUIDES AND TOURS

Tour companies offer a broad choice of excursions, from half a day in Sydney to long-haul journeys into the Outback. Harbour cruises range from the general sightseeing tours to specialised visits to historic Fort Denison. There are also local walking tours, and tours for cyclists, wildlife-lovers and others with special interests. A hop-on tour bus circulates around the popular sites in Sydney, for a daily fee, and there's a similar ferry service (see Sydney Visitor Centre, page 130).

H

HEALTH AND MEDICAL CARE

Standards of hygiene are high, particularly in food preparation. Doctors and dentists are proficient and hospitals well equipped. If you fall ill, your hotel can call a doctor or refer you to one, or you can ask your embassy, high commission or consulate for a list of approved doctors. You should take out health insurance before departure to cover your stay. Also ensure you have personal insurance or travel insurance with a health component to cover the possibility of illness or accident.

You are allowed to bring 'reasonable quantities' of prescribed non-narcotic medications. All should be clearly labelled and identifiable and carried in personal hand luggage. For large quantities, bring a doctor's certificate to produce at Customs if necessary. Local pharmacies can fill prescriptions written by an Australian-registered doctor.

Health hazards. Ultraviolet levels are very high in Australia; high-factor protective cream is essential if exposed, even on cloudy days.

Although there are poisonous snakes and spiders in Australia, you are unlikely to encounter them in central Sydney; they sometimes crop up in the outer suburbs. The brown snake, whose venom is the second-most deadly in the world, is the most dangerous. They are generally not found in central Sydney, but routinely slither around farms, the bush and suburbs. The Sydney funnelweb spider, dark and bulbous, is one of the world's most lethal. An antivenom has been developed. The spider lives in holes in the ground, chiefly in Sydney's northern suburbs. Bites are very rare and require immediate medical attention. Catch the spider for identification if you can. Other poisonous spiders include the redback, the eastern mouse spider and the white-tail. Bites from these are rare and seldom lethal, but see a doctor if bitten.

Shark attacks are extremely rare. In certain seasons and areas, bluebottles (also called Portuguese man o' war) may cluster. The sting is painful but can be treated with hot (not boiling) water. Many bathing areas have kiosks with first-aid supplies for jellyfish stings.

Sydney has Australia's highest rate of AIDS-related deaths, so protect yourself from exposure to sexually transmitted diseases.

L

LANGUAGE

English is spoken everywhere. The vernacular is sometimes called Strine, which is how the word 'Australian' sounds in an extreme Australian pronunciation. Educated and cultivated Australians tend to speak in more neutral tones; it sounds more like middle-class British than Crocodile Dundee. Foreigners who listen carefully usually understand what's said, at least when it's repeated.

LGBTQ TRAVELLERS

There is a huge gay community in Sydney. NSW has outlawed discrimination against gay people, but intolerance to some degree still exists.

The main gay weekly publication is the *Sydney Star Observer*. Obtainable from bookshops, pubs and cafés throughout inner Sydney, it contains news and information on gay events and venues. Sydney's main gay district is Oxford Street and the surrounding Darlinghurst area. Another neighbourhood with a fairly strong gay scene is King Street in

Newtown. Well-known pubs around Oxford Street favoured by the male gay community include the Beauchamp, the Oxford and the Beresford. In Newtown, men congregate at the Imperial Hotel and the Newtown Hotel, while lesbians hang out at the Bank Hotel.

M

MAPS

State and local tourist offices give away useful maps of their areas, and there are free specialised maps, of Darling Harbour, for instance, or the Sydney ferry network. Car-hire companies often supply free city directories showing each street and place of interest. For more detailed maps, it may be worth buying a Gregory's Street Directory.

MEDIA

Newspapers. Sydney's biggest-selling daily, the *Sydney Morning Herald*, publishes a TV guide on Mondays, a restaurant and cooking guide called Good Food on Tuesdays, and an entertainment guide called Shortlist on Fridays. Other daily papers are the *Daily Telegraph*, the *Australian* and the *Australian Financial Review*. The last two circulate nationally. Specialist newsstands in Sydney sell newspapers from New York, London, Rome, Paris, Hong Kong and Singapore.

Television. There are over a dozen broadcast TV channels. Australian Broadcasting Corporation and Special Broadcasting Service are both taxpayer-funded and commercial-free. SBS has a schedule of documentaries, overseas programming and foreign films with subtitles. Cable television is widely available in Sydney, as are subscription TV services. In many remote areas, the National Indigenous Television Service provides programming by and for Australia's native peoples.

Radio. Sydney radio is as lively and varied as the city itself. Both the AM and FM frequencies have commercial and taxpayer-funded (and therefore commercial-free) stations. In addition, there is a plethora of low-powered FM stations serving neighbourhoods, small towns and ethnic groups. There's also a handful of internet stations (see www.sydneymusicweb.com to find a specific format and frequency).

MONEY

Currency. Banknotes (bills) feature transparent panels instead of watermarks. The currency is decimal-based, with the dollar as the basic unit (100 cents equals one dollar). Notes come in $100, $50, $20, $10 and $5 denominations. Coins come in 5c, 10c, 20c, 50c, $1 and $2 denominations. Because there are no 1- or 2-cent pieces, when giving change prices are rounded to the nearest 5 cents. As for credit cards, American Express, MasterCard, Visa, Carte Blanche, Bankcard and Diners Club are widely accepted, but the Discover Card is not. You may have problems using credit cards in smaller towns, shops and country areas. Some businesses impose a small credit-card surcharge.

Currency exchange. All international airports in Australia provide currency exchange facilities, and foreign notes or travellers' cheques can be converted at most banks. Cash travellers' cheques at banks or larger hotels, as it may be difficult elsewhere. Some banks may charge a fee for cashing them – Australian banks charge for just about everything these days. The most popular cheques are American Express, Thomas Cook, Barclays, Bank of America, Visa and MasterCard.

ATMs. The facility to use ATM machines to perform currency exchanges and to withdraw Australian dollars has reduced the need for traveller's cheques. Your card must be part of the CIRRUS, PLUS, STAR, Interlink or Maestro POS network to have international access. Debit cards are widely used. Electronic point-of-sale transactions (EFTPOS) are increasingly common, even in more remote areas.

O

OPENING TIMES

Banks. Generally open 9.30am–4pm Mon–Thu and 9.30am–5pm on Fridays. Selected banking facilities may be available on Saturday morning.

Currency exchanges at Sydney Airport are open all hours.

Post offices. 9am–5pm Mon–Fri; some open Saturday morning.

Shops. The big department stores are open 9am–5.30pm Mon to Fri and 9am–6pm on Saturday and 10/11am–5pm on Sunday. Thursday is late shopping night, when stores stay open until 8 or 9pm. Stores in some suburbs are open late on other nights. Shopping centres such as the Queen Victoria Building and Harbourside are open seven days a week.

Bars/pubs/hotels. Licensing hours vary, but a typical schedule would be 10am–10pm or 11pm Mon–Sat, with most pubs open by noon on Sunday as well. Nightclubs can stay open until the next morning, if the clientele can make it.

P

POLICE

NSW operates its own police force, covering both urban and rural areas. The Australian Federal Police, based in Canberra, has jurisdiction over government property, including airports, and deals with interstate problems. Sydney police are generally helpful and friendly. The emergency number is 000. From a mobile, 112 and 911 also work.

POST OFFICES

Post offices are signposted 'Australia Post'. Most open 9am–5pm Mon–Fri, though some suburban offices open on Saturday morning, and the General Post Office (GPO) in Pitt Street near Martin Place is open 8.30am–5.30pm Tue–Fri and 10am–2pm Saturday. This is the main post office for poste restante – take ID to pick it up.

Postcards or greeting cards to the US or Europe cost AU$3 and take about a week to arrive. Letters of up to 70g cost from AU$3 and arrive in 9 business days. Local letters cost $1. Stamps are often available at hotels and some retail outlets. Postboxes are red with an Australia Post logo. Most post offices and hotels have fax facilities.

PUBLIC HOLIDAYS

1 January New Year's Day
26 January Australia Day
March/April Good Friday, Holy Saturday, Easter Monday
25 April Anzac Day
June (2nd Monday) Queen's Birthday
October (1st Monday) Labour Day
25 December Christmas Day
26 December Boxing Day

School holidays are four times a year, the longest one being in the summer through the latter part of December and all January.

T

TELEPHONE

Australia's country code is 61, and the code for Sydney is 2. To call a Sydney number from another country, dial your country's international access code, then 612, then the eight-digit number. Australia's telephone network, run by Telstra, is sophisticated; you can dial anywhere in the country from almost any phone and expect a clear line. Many hotel rooms have phones from which you can dial cross-country (STD) or internationally (IDD) (but be careful of the surcharges).

Cell phone service is generally available throughout much of Australia, including many of the more remote areas. Unless your phone contract includes international service, you can end up paying huge roaming fees or not have service at all. An economical option is to rent or buy a cell phone or an Australian SIM card for a GSM phone. GSM phones are standard in Europe and the UK; they are uncommon in the US. They allow for inserting SIM cards for each country you visit.

You'll find payphones in railway and bus stations, government buildings, some shopping centres and at the odd major intersection. The minimum cost of a local public payphone call is 50 cents. Long-distance calls within Australia and International Direct Dialling calls can be made on Telstra public payphones. Check with the operator for these charges, as they vary for distances and the time of day. Some public payphones take all Australian coins, others do not accept the smaller denominations and some only accept phonecards. Pre-paid cards are used to make local, STD and IDD calls. Phonecards are widely sold at newsagents and other shops, and come in denominations of $10 and $20. The Telstra PhoneAway pre-paid card enables you to use virtually any phone in Australia – all call costs are charged against the card. Credit phones, found at airports, many hotels and several city-centre locations, accept most major credit cards such as American Express, MasterCard and Visa. To make a reverse-charge (call collect) call, see www.telstra.com.au .

To reach an overseas number, dial 0011, then the country code of the destination, the area code and the local number.

TIME ZONES

Australia has three time zones: New South Wales and Australian Capital Territory operate on Eastern Standard Time (EST). Daylight saving (where the clocks go forward an hour) runs in New South Wales and Australian Capital Territory from the end of October to the first Sunday in April. Some places don't follow the time switch, though, so you may want to check locally. The chart below shows the time differences between Sydney and various other cities in January and July:

	Los Angeles	New York	London	**Sydney**	Auckland
Jan					
	3pm	6pm	11pm	**10am**	noon
	Fri	Fri	Fri	**Sat**	Sat
July					
	5pm	8pm	1am	**10am**	noon
	Fri	Fri	Sat	**Sat**	Sat

TIPPING

Tipping is an optional gratuity for good service. If service is poor or a waiter is surly, don't tip. It is not customary to tip taxi drivers, porters at airports or hairdressers. Porters have set charges at railway terminals, but not at hotels. Hotels and restaurants do not usually add service charges to accounts, although some restaurants and cafés add a 10 percent for service on public holidays. In better-class restaurants, patrons sometimes tip food and drink waiters up to 10 percent of the bill, but only if service is good (if it's very good, make it 15 percent).

TOILETS

'Dunny' is the Outback slang term for a toilet, but 'washroom' and 'restrooms' are all understood. In Sydney, public toilets are often locked after certain hours, but you can use pub or store facilities without making a purchase. Toilets are usually clean, even in the Outback.

TOURIST INFORMATION

To obtain tourist information before you leave home, see the Tourism Australia website (www.australia.com); contact the head office: ask.us@tourism.australia.com; tel: 02 9360-1111; or visit an overseas office:

Canada: 2 Bloor Street West, Suite 2601, Toronto, ON, M4W3E2, tel: (416) 935-1896, ext. 226.

New Zealand: Jenny Aitken, General Manager NZ, tel: 64-9- 377-5348, jaitken@tourism.australia.com.

UK: Australia Centre, Australia House, 6th Floor, Melbourne Place/ Strand, London WC2B 4LG, tel: (020) 7438-4600.

US: Mailbox #358, 2029 Century Park, E Ste 3150, Los Angeles CA 90067, tel: (310) 695-3200.

Once in Sydney, visit the Sydney Visitor Centre (www.sydneyvisitorcentre.com), in two locations:

The Rocks: Corner of Argyle and Playfair streets, daily 9.30am–5.30pm, tel: 1800 067-676.

Kings Cross: information kiosk corner of Darlinghurst Road and Springfield Avenue, Potts Point, daily 9.30am–5pm, tel: 02 9265 9333.

TRANSPORT

Sydney has a clean, safe, easy to use and efficient public transport system. You can also combine transport with admission to attractions and various other discounts. For information on Sydney's public ferries, buses and trains, call 131-500. The NSW Transport website allows you to search for train, bus and ferry schedules: www.transportnsw.info.

For all Sydney public transport services, including Sydney trains and NSW TrainLink intercity trains, all buses in Sydney, Blue Mountains, Central Coast, Hunter and Illawarra, all Sydney ferries and the Stockton ferry in Newcastle, and light rail, you need an **Opal card** or an Opal single ticket.

The Opal cards daily cap for adults is AU$15.80 or AU$63.20 for a week. Opal cards can be bought online (www.opal.com.au) or at newsagents or service desks. The card should be tapped on the reader at the start and end of every journey.

Buses. Buses are a practical option during business hours, but service tapers off after dark. The two main starting points for buses are at Wynyard Park on York Street (for the northern suburbs) and at Circular Quay (all other directions). Bus route numbers starting with an 'L' are express services with limited stops. Wheelchair-accessible buses show the international access symbol. The NSW Transport website and hotline has detailed information. Big Bus Tours Hop-On Hop-Off (www.bigbustours.com) service offers two routes: the City Tour and the Bondi Tour, both are great value. The first covers all the main central Sydney sights and the second visits the bays, beaches and attractions of the eastern side of town, including Kings Cross and Watsons Bay. They run a continuous loop (with narration) throughout the day and evening. Your ticket allows you to hop on and off as often as you like. A one-day ticket is AU$55; a two-day option is AU$ 75.

Railway. Sydney's underground railway system (subway) operates from 4.30am to midnight; it's the central unit of a railway network that stretches out to the suburbs. After midnight, the Nightride bus service takes over and runs through the night. Sydney's trains are double-deck, and station platforms are marked with special 'Night safe' areas, to show you which carriages are open; others may be closed after dark.

Light rail. The 'light rail' system in Sydney is actually a tram service. It runs from Central Station through Chinatown and Darling Harbour to the Fish Market and a little beyond. A new line is currently under construction that will run from Circular Quay along George Street to Central Station, then on to Surry Hills, Moore Park, Randwick and and Kingsford. This is due to open in 2020.

Ferries. A vital part of life in Sydney, with so many commuters continually criss-crossing the harbour, ferries sail between 6am and 11pm daily. Most depart from Circular Quay, providing inexpensive outings for sightseers to Kirribilli, Taronga Zoo, Manly and Darling Harbour. Water taxis are easy to use but are expensive (tel: 0414 708-020 or 1800 326-822).

Taxis. You can hail a cab on the street if the orange light on top is lit. Otherwise, go to one of the taxi ranks at shopping centres, transport terminals or big hotels, and take the first taxi in the rank. Or phone for a taxi; tel: 132 227 or 13 10 17. Zero 2000, a wheelchair-accessible taxi service, can be contacted on 02 8332-0200. There are also several 'secure' taxi stands which are supervised in the wee hours. Meters indicate the fare plus any extras, such as waiting time. Higher tariffs apply 10pm–6am. It is not customary to tip taxi drivers.

V

VISA AND ENTRY REQUIREMENTS

Australia requires all visitors to hold a visa. Citizens of New Zealand receive an automatic electronic visa when they present their passports at the Immigration counter. The visa you need depends on what your visit is for, and how long you plan to stay.

Tourist stream visitor visa (subclass 600, from AUD$140) allows you to visit Australia for up to 12 months. You are not allowed to work. Electronic Travel Authority ETA (subclass 601) allows you to enter Australia as many times as you want, for up to three months at a time, for up to 12 months. The service fee is $20. eVisitor (subclass 651) is for people who hold passports from certain countries (free visa). You may enter Australia as many times you wish, for up to three months at a time, for up to 12 months after the visa is granted. Special category visa (subclass 444) is for the NZ citizens. Working holiday visa (subclass 417) is for young people between 18–31 years of age, up to 35 if you are a Canadian or Irish citizen. You must apply for it outside Australia. You can only work six months with one employer. More information about other visa types can be found on www.immi.homeaffairs.gov.au.

Australia operates reciprocal working holiday schemes with Canada, Ireland, Japan, Korea, Malta, the Netherlands, France, Germany, Denmark, Sweden, Norway, the UK and some other countries, for applicants between 18 and 31 (up to 35 for Canadian and Irish citizens).

Entry formalities. On the last leg of your flight to Australia you'll be asked to complete a Customs form, swearing that you are not trying to import foreign foodstuffs (including fresh fruit), weapons, drugs or other forbidden articles.

There is also an Immigration form. Vaccinations are not required unless you have come from or visited a yellow fever-infected country or zone within six days prior to arrival. You may be required to show your return or onward ticket, and you may need to prove that your funds are sufficient to last out your planned stay. Sniffer dogs are used in the baggage reclaim area to detect items.

Exit formalities. You'll need to fill out a departure form for the Immigration authorities. If you are carrying AU$10,000 or more in foreign currency, you must declare it to Customs.

Duty-free. Anyone over the age of 18 is allowed to bring into Australia AU$900 worth of goods not including alcohol or tobacco, 2.25 litres of alcohol (including wine, beer or spirits) and 50 cigarettes or 50g of cigars or tobacco products other than cigarettes.

W

WEBSITES AND INTERNET ACCESS

Internet access is almost universal. Several places offer free Wi-Fi, including the ferries. Libraries also allow you to use their computers. There is a comprehensive list of free Wi-Fi spots at www.freewifi.com. au or www.openwifispots.com. Broadband is offered in rural areas.

Australian Tourist Commission: www.australia.com

Darling Harbour: www.darlingharbour.com

National Parks in NSW: www.nationalparks.nsw.gov.au

Public transport information: www.transportnsw.info

Sydney City Council: www.cityofsydney.com.au

Sydney information finder: www.sydney.com

Sydney Morning Herald: www.smh.com.au

Sydney Visitor Centre: www.sydney.com

Tourism New South Wales: www.visitnsw.com.au

Y

YOUTH HOSTELS

There are two types of hostel accommodation: privately owned backpacker hostels and YHA Hostels. Both provide self-catering accommodation from about AU$30 a night. Hostels are open to all ages. Some have private, semi-private and family rooms. See www.yha.com.au.

Sydney's Song Hotels (www.songhotels.com.au) are associated with YWCA, but you do not need to be young, a woman or Christian to stay. From AU$100.

RECOMMENDED HOTELS

Sydney has a wide range of accommodation to suit travellers. You will find everything from elegant luxury five-star hotels with impeccable service to self-contained apartment hotels, to back-to-basics, inexpensive hostels. It is worth noting that you may find that rates tend to fall sharply once you move inland from the popular harbourside neighbourhoods.

The symbols below are a guide to the price of a standard double room with bath or shower, excluding tips; breakfast is not included unless otherwise stated. Prices are based on double occupancy on a midweek night. Many hotels in Sydney offer discount packages and deals which can be substantial. Check online to see what's on offer, or ask when making reservations. All hotels take major credit cards unless otherwise stated. For more information about accommodation in Sydney, see page 115.

$$$$	over AU$300
$$$	AU$200–300
$$	AU$120–200
$	below AU$120

THE ROCKS AND CIRCULAR QUAY

The Rocks and Circular Quay are the epicentre for tourists in Sydney: everyone wants to stay there and the hotel prices reflect this. You'll have the choice between modern mega-towers that could be anywhere in the world and more intimate boutiques, in century-old buildings, that lie in their shadows.

Australian Hotel $$ *100 Cumberland Street, The Rocks, tel: 02 9247-2229*, www.australianheritagehotel.com. A lovely old pub (with perhaps the most extensive list of brews in Sydney) built in 1913, with very comfortable rooms offering an inexpensive B&B accommodation option in The Rocks. Bathrooms are shared. The roof terrace has views of the Harbour Bridge and Opera House. Price includes breakfast. 18 rooms.

Bed and Breakfast Sydney Harbour $$$ *140–142 Cumberland Street, The Rocks, tel: 02 9247-1130*, www.bbsydneyharbour.com.au. This restored early 20th-century building is located around the corner from the busiest part of The Rocks, and within a 10-minute walk of Circular Quay. The rooms, some of which have harbour views, are nicely fitted out with period furniture, queen-size beds, and most have their own bathroom. The three-course cooked breakfasts (included in the price) are served in the tree-shaded private courtyard. 9 rooms.

Four Seasons $$$$ *199 George Street, tel: 02 9250-3100*, www.foursea sons.com/sydney. One of Sydney's original five-star hotels, the Four Seasons has a superlative reputation. Personal service is great; the hotel overlooks the harbour and The Rocks district. Wheelchair access. 620 rooms.

Glenferrie Lodge Hotel, Kirribilli $$ *12A Carabella Street, Kirribilli, tel: 02 9955-1685*, www.glenferrielodge.com. What a difference a harbour makes. The six-minute ferry jaunt from Circular Quay to Kirribilli earns you a room with a balcony overlooking the Opera House, Bridge and Quay at about a quarter of the price of rooms on the other side of the harbour. Simple, comfortable rooms; all share bathrooms. Very friendly staff and a hot breakfast buffet every morning. It's consistently voted one of the best budget deals in Sydney. 70 rooms from single to family. Pets are welcome with some conditions.

Harbour Rocks Hotel $$$ *34 Harringon Street, tel: 02 8220-9999*, www.harbourrocks.com.au. A real find. Moderately priced (for The Rocks), well appointed and perfectly situated four-star boutique property. Some rooms in the 150-year-old building overlook the harbour. 55 rooms.

Holiday Inn Old Sydney $$$$ *55 George Street, tel: 1800-770-199 or 02 9255-1800*, www.ihg.com. Great location in The Rocks, with rooftop heated swimming pool overlooking the harbour and Opera

House, sauna, spa and secure undercover parking. Wheelchair access. 174 guest rooms.

Hotel InterContinental Sydney $$$$ *117 Macquarie Street, NSW 2000, tel: 02 9253-9000*, www.ihg.com/intercontinental. In an elegant building that incorporates Sydney's historic Treasury Building, the InterContinental combines 19th-century grace with 21st-century comfort. Located on one of the city's stateliest thoroughfares, and within walking distance of the harbour, the Opera House and the Royal Botanic Gardens. Swimming pool, health club, sauna and non-smoking floors. Wheelchair access. 509 rooms, 28 suites.

The Langham Hotel $$$$ *89–113 Kent Street, Millers Point, tel: 02 9256-2222*, www.langhamhotels.com.au. One of the grandest and most luxurious hotels in Sydney. Once owned by the Orient Express, it has the aura of European grand hotels, although it was built in the 1990s. It offers a day spa, indoor pool and five-star restaurant. It's pet-friendly (extra charge); dogs have a good choice of meals from the Scooby Doo room service menu. It is within easy walking distance of The Rocks and Circular Quay. Wheelchair access. 77 rooms.

The Russell Hotel $$$ *143 George Street, tel: 02 9241-3543*, www.therussell.com.au. Very comfortable hotel which takes advantage of the high ceilings and architecture of the 1887 building. Furnishings – many of them antiques – reflect the period. Rooftop garden overlooks the harbour; street-side balcony looks down upon George Street. Most rooms have en suite bathrooms; all have ceiling fans, hairdryers, bathrobes. The rate includes a continental breakfast.

Sir Stamford at Circular Quay $$$$ *93 Macquarie Street, tel: 02 9252-4600*, www.stamford.com.au. Very elegant and a nice choice for a very upscale lodging a bit away from the heart of The Rocks. Opposite the Royal Botanic Gardens and filled with oil paintings, Persian rugs and similar clubby trappings. Wheelchair access. 105 rooms.

Youth Hostel, The Rocks $$ *110 Cumberland Street, tel: 02 8272-0900*, www.yha.com.au. Around the corner from some of the most expensive hotel rooms in Sydney, the youth hostel provides safe, comfortable, convenient accommodation for tourists and families as well as backpackers. As with all hostels, 'shared' rooms means strangers rooming together, but you have the option of a private room for a higher price. This hostel also has family rooms for up to six people.

CITY CENTRE

1831 Boutique Hotel $$ *631–5 George Street, tel: 02 9265-8888*, www.1831.com.au. The rooms here are a bit small and it is important to note that the noise from the street can be heard in street-facing rooms, but the staff are famous for their friendly attitude and eagerness to make your visit memorable. There is a guest lounge which is a particularly relaxing sitting area with a library and communal kitchenette. The free CBD shuttle stops at the front door.

Mercure Hotel Sydney on Broadway $$$ *818–820 George Street, tel: 02 9217-6666*, www.mercuresydney.com.au. On the western side of the CBD near Prince Alfred and Hyde parks. Contemporary decor throughout. The fitness centre with pool, gym and sauna is on the rooftop, providing a great view as an incentive to work out. Wheelchair access. 517 rooms.

Oaks Hyde Park Plaza $$$ *38 College Street, tel: 02 9331-6933*, www.oakshotels.com. Overlooking the park with Oxford Street just around the corner, this hotel offers a variety of self-contained apartments, ranging from studios to two-bedroom family suites and three-bedroom executive suites. Rooms are generally about twice the size of other hotel rooms. Some have balconies overlooking the park and city. There's also a heated pool, spa, sauna and gym. Wheelchair access. 182 rooms.

Pullman Sydney Hyde Park $$$$ *36 College Street, tel: 02 9361-8400*, www.pullmansydneyhydepark.com.au. Situated opposite the famous Hyde Park in the epicentre of the arts, retail and business district. The outdoor rooftop pool offers stunning views over Hyde Park. 241 rooms.

Rydges World Square $$$ *389 Pitt Street, tel: 02 8268-1888*, www.rydges. com. This hotel is adjacent to the World Square Shopping Centre. It is highly regarded for its 'green' environmental design and operation. 450 rooms.

Sheraton Grand Sydney Hyde Park $$$$ *161 Elizabeth Street, tel: 02 9286-6000*, www.marriott.com. No harbour views, but you can gaze out on the verdant foliage of Hyde Park from the upper floors of this five-star hotel. The grand lobby and sweeping staircases are complemented by a modern health club and gym. Slick contemporary decor. Conveniently located near Sydney's prime shopping venues and department stores. Wheelchair access. 558 rooms.

Sydney Boulevard Hotel $$$ *90 William Street, tel: 02 9383-7222*, www. sydneyboulevard.com.au. Four-star property with wonderful views of Hyde Park and the city skyline. Contemporary decor and feel. Centrally located in the CBD, a short walk to shopping and entertainment. Very popular with business travellers. Restaurant on the 25th floor has a great view. 271 rooms.

Sydney Central YHA $$ *Pitt Street and Rawson Place, NSW 2000, tel: 02 9218-9000*, www.yha.com.au. Technically a youth hostel, it's also an excellent, centrally located hotel in a heritage building opposite Central Station. Most rooms are dormitory-style: they are comfortable, but you will be rooming with strangers and sharing a bathroom. However, they are around AU$50 a night and are safe and clean. Private rooms run to about AU$130. The YHA also has a pool, sauna, laundry and self-catering kitchens. Wheelchair access. 144 rooms.

DARLING HARBOUR

Adina Apartment Hotel $$$ *55 Shelley Street, King Street Wharf, Darling Harbour, tel: 02 9249-7000*, www.adinahotels.com.sydney. Air-conditioned studios and apartments, most with private balcony overlooking Cockle Bay. 114 rooms.

Hotel Ibis Darling Harbour $$$ *70 Murray Street, Pyrmont NSW 2009, tel: 02 9563-0888*, www.accorhotels.com. A quick walk from the attractions of Darling Harbour and Cockle Bay Wharf, and the Sydney Light Rail train stop at the hotel door. Easy access to Star City Casino, city-centre shopping and entertainment, Chinatown and Central Station. Wheelchair access. 256 rooms. Non-smoking.

Hyatt Regency $$$$ *161 Sussex Street, NSW 2000, tel: 02 8099-1234,* www.hyatt.com. Australia's largest hotel – its elegant, curved shape facing Darling Harbour belies its size. The Hyatt Regency is a short walk from the CBD and Sydney entertainment venues. 892 rooms.

Vulcan Hotel $$$ *500 Wattle Street, Ultimo, NSW 2007, tel: 02 9211-3283,* www.vulcanhotel.com.au. Winner of the 'Best Boutique Hotel in Sydney'. 46 rooms in a lovingly restored 1894 building that's a short stroll from Darling Harbour and the entertainment district. Contemporary accommodation with everything a traveller needs.

Woolbrokers Hotel $$ *22 Allen Street, Pyrmont, tel: 02 9552- 4773,* www. woolbrokershotel.com.au. Very basic, two-star, B&B-style hotel in the heart of Darling Harbour. No air conditioning or lift, and most of the rooms share a bathroom. But the friendly staff, fantastic location and price are worth the inconvenience. 27 rooms.

EASTERN SUBURBS

City Crown Motel $$ *289 Crown Street, Surry Hills, NSW 2010, tel: 02 9331-2433,* www.citycrownmotel.com.au. A trim, pleasant, family-run property in a trendy street in inner-city Surry Hills, a short stroll from Oxford Street and with plenty of cafés and restaurants around. All rooms have their own bathroom and balcony. 30 rooms.

De Vere Hotel $$ *44–46 Macleay Street, Potts Point NSW 2011, tel: 02 9358-1211,* www.devere.com.au. A good, comfortable budget choice in the heart of the Potts Point/Kings Cross entertainment district, and close to city attractions. Some rooms on upper floors have harbour views. Full range of rooms from budget single to family studios. 117 rooms.

Hotel 59 $$ *59 Bayswater Road, Kings Cross NSW 2011, tel: 02 9360-5900,* www.hotel59.com.au. A family-owned and run European-style B&B with only nine rooms. It is located in a quiet section of Bayswater Road. Fairly basic rooms all have private baths. It's spotlessly clean and known for its excellent cooked breakfasts.

Medusa $$$$ *267 Darlinghurst Road, Darlinghurst, NSW 2010, tel: 02 9331-1000*, www.medusa.com.au. Perhaps the most trendy and glamorous boutique hotel in Sydney. 18 rooms decorated in very modern, avant-garde design. Staff are every bit as attentive as you would expect in such an intimate property. The reflection pool in the courtyard is delightful.

Rydges Sydney Central $$$ *28 Albion Street, Surry Hills, tel: 02 9289-0000*, www.rydges.com. The hotel has a clean, modern vibe. There are spacious rooms and updated bathrooms. A good work desk and space make it a perfect choice for business travellers. Wheelchair access. 309 rooms.

Victoria Court Sydney $$$ *122 Victoria Street, Potts Point NSW 2011, tel: 02 9357-3200*. Wonderfully charming B&B in 1881 building located on a quiet, leafy street in Potts Point. Depending on the room, you may have a marble fireplace, balcony or four-poster bed. All of the rooms have en suite bathrooms. Many good cafés and restaurants are nearby. 22 rooms.

THE BEACHES
Bondi

Hotel Bondi $$ *178 Campbell Parade, Bondi Beach, tel: 02 9130-3271*, www.hotelbondi.com.au. A Bondi landmark for 90 years. The closest hotel to the beach, its oceanfront rooms have breathtaking views. It's surrounded by shops and restaurants.

Ravesi's $$$$ *Corner of Campbell Parade & Hall Street, Bondi Beach NSW 2026, tel: 02 9365-4422*, www.ravesis.com.au. Walk across to the beach for a morning swim from this lovely Bondi beachfront boutique hotel. Rooms are stylishly decorated and vary from compact rooms with no view to suites with a terrace overlooking the ocean. The hotel's restaurant serves very good cocktails. 12 rooms.

QT Bondi $$$$ *6 Beach Road, Bondi Beach, NSW 2016; tel: 02-8362-3900*, www.qthotelsandresorts.com. QT offers the only boutique hotel apartments on Bondi Beach. Experience a mix of Bondi barefoot luxury and the creature comforts you would expect to find in a world-class hotel.

Manly

Novotel Sydney Manly Pacific $$$$ *55 North Steyne, Manly, tel: 02 9977-7666*, www.novotel.accorhotels.com. Fabulous beachfront location with easy access to the ferry terminal and a short walk to Manly Corso where a wide range of restaurants, shops and bars reside.

INDEX

INSIGHT ⊙ GUIDES POCKET GUIDE

SYDNEY

First Edition 2019

Editor: Sian Marsh
Author: Ken Bernstein
Head of DTP and Pre-Press: Rebeka Davies
Managing Editor: Carine Tracanelli
Picture Editor: Tom Smyth
Cartography Update: Carte
Update Production: Apa Digital
Photography Credits: Alamy 1, 59, 63;
Corbis 94; Getty Images 4MC, 22, 71, 81;
Glyn Genin/Apa Publications 4TC, 6L, 7, 7R,
33, 34, 37, 44, 46, 72, 84, 87, 93, 107; iStock
5MC, 11, 12, 43, 60, 67, 73, 75; Jerry Dennis/
Apa Publications 89; Public domain 14,
16, 19; Shutterstock 4ML, 5TC, 5M, 5MC,
5M, 6R, 21, 30, 40, 49, 51, 52, 55, 64, 68, 82;
Tourism New South Wales 4TL, 4/5T, 26, 29,
39, 56, 76, 78, 90, 97, 101, 103, 104
Cover Picture: iStock

Distribution
UK, Ireland and Europe: Apa Publications
(UK) Ltd; sales@insightguides.com
United States and Canada: Ingram
Publisher Services; ips@ingramcontent.com
Australia and New Zealand: Woodslane;
info@woodslane.com.au
Southeast Asia: Apa Publications (SN) Pte;
singaporeoffice@insightguides.com
Worldwide: Apa Publications (UK) Ltd;
sales@insightguides.com

Special Sales, Content Licensing and CoPublishing
Insight Guides can be purchased in bulk
quantities at discounted prices. We can
create special editions, personalised jackets
and corporate imprints tailored to your
needs. sales@insightguides.com;
www.insightguides.biz

Contact us
Every effort has been made to provide
accurate information in this publication,
but changes are inevitable. The publisher
cannot be responsible for any resulting loss,
inconvenience or injury. We would appreciate
it if readers would call our attention to any
errors or outdated information. We also
welcome your suggestions; please contact
us at: hello@insightguides.com
www.insightguides.com